UNWIND BY WATER IN LAKELAND

MARTIN WILSON

© **Copyright** Martin Wilson, 2002

Published by Cygnet Publishing

ISBN: 0-9540608-0-6

Cover photograph: Shoreline adjacent to Mossdale Bay, Ullswater

Printed by: Cypher Digital Print, Milnthorpe, LA7 7AD

CONTENTS

		Page
Site location map		4
Introduction		5
Site format		7
Site hazards		8
The Lakes		9
Bassenthwaite Lake		10
1	Hursthole Point & Blackstock Point	11
2	Ouse Bridge	13
Buttermere		15
3	South-West shore	16
4	North-East shore	19
Coniston Water		22
5	Lake Road, Coniston	23
6	Brown Howe	25
7	Blawith Common	27
8	Low Peel Near & High Peel Near	29
9	Eastern shore	31
Crummock Water		34
10	Mill Beck	35
11	Rannerdale	37
12	Low Ling Crag	39
13	Lanthwaite Wood	41

		Page
Derwent Water		43
14	Western shore	44
15	Barrow Bay to Kettlewell	47
16	Calfclose Bay	50
17	Friar's Crag/Strandshag Bay	52
18	Crow Park	54
Grasmere		56
19	Grasmere	57
Rydal Water		59
20	Rydal Water	60
Ullswater		62
21	Glenridding	63
22	Mossdale Bay	66
23	Glencoyne	68
24	North Glencoyne	70
25	Aira Point	72
26	Beneath Gowbarrow	74
27	Gowbarrow	76
28	Sandwick Bay	78
Wast Water		80
29	Overbeck Bridge	81
30	Netherbeck Bridge	83
31	North-West shore	86
32	Wasdale Hall	89

		Page
Windermere		91
33	Borrans Park	92
34	Jenkin Field	94
35	Brockhole	96
36	Wray Castle	98
37	Red Nab	100
38	Rayrigg Meadow/Millerground	102
39	Cockshott Point	105
40	Coatlap Point	107
41	Beech Hill	109
42	Fell Foot	111
The Rivers		113
43	Barrow Beck at Ashness Bridge	114
44	River Derwent at Grange-in-Borrowdale	116
45	River Duddon at Birks Bridge	119
46	River Esk at Forge Bridge	121
47	River Mite at Miterdale	123
48	River Rothay at White Moss Common	125
49	Watendlath Beck at Watendlath	127
50	Yewdale Beck at Tilberthwaite	129

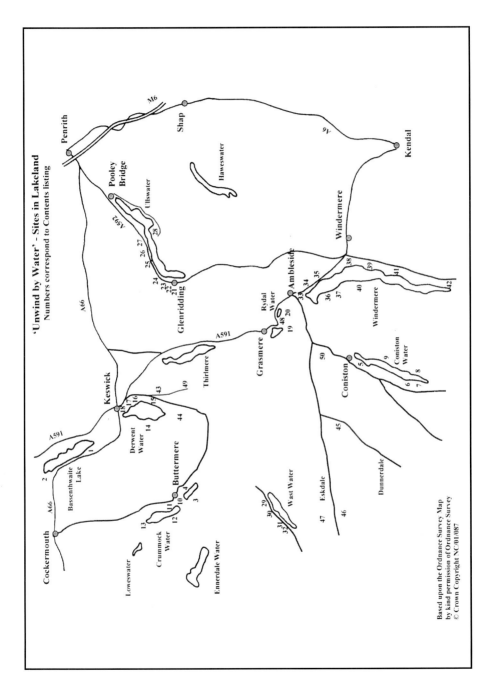

'Unwind by Water' - Sites in Lakeland
Numbers correspond to Contents listing

Based upon the Ordnance Survey Map
by kind permission of Ordnance Survey
© Crown Copyright NC/01/087

4

Introduction

Surely anyone who has ever been to the Lake District on a lovely day has noticed just how attractive the lakes and rivers look. Beautiful shimmering lakes and crystal clear babbling becks epitomize tranquillity and the idea of a relaxing few hours spent unwinding by the water, with pastimes such as picnicking, sunbathing, playing, paddling and bathing on offer, must be very appealing in anybody's view.

Many people come to the Lake District to do some exploring and walking but this can be exhausting and the option of taking some time out to unwind by the water surrounded by the beauty of the Lake District is an experience not to be missed.

Those with children will be slightly restricted anyway, but youngsters like nothing better than playing around in and near water and a few hours spent by the lake or river will certainly be appreciated by all the family.

Yes of course the Lake District has a slight reputation for the odd bit of bad weather, but despite this there are still plenty of days in the year when it is dry and warm enough to sit and picnic outdoors and also to paddle or bathe in the lakes and rivers of the area.

Many people have a favourite place where they like to spend some time by the water but there are often more suitable sites that you may not know about. There are some real hidden gems in the Lakes which have great shorelines, magnificent views and good access but the trick is knowing where these places are.

This book describes 50 of the more popular sites in terms of parking, access, suitability for relaxing, picnicking, paddling, bathing and playing and also gives indications of sunshine and shade expectations. You may not have realised that there are so many waterside access areas and some are certainly off the beaten track but all are recognised recreational areas and all have their own appeal. Most of the sites are on the lakes but there are a number located on rivers which can be equally popular and just as enjoyable.

The book describes the appeal of each site so that people can easily ascertain if a particular site is suitable for them. Depending on circumstances people will often have different needs and requirements of a site and the book is structured to highlight these. For example a family with very young children might not

5

need masses of space but closeness to the car and facilities on site with some shade might be important. A family with older children will probably want some good open areas, which are preferably grassy, where they can run around and play games. A couple on their own may just want a quiet place to sit and relax by the water and take in the great surroundings. All sites certainly have different appeals and there is enough choice in the book to suit all needs and requirements.

The sites have mostly been chosen as being quite easily accessible from a car park appreciating the difficulty of days out with the family and the amount of kit that is often needed. Some sites do involve a bit of a walk but these tend to be more peaceful and tranquil thus making the walk worthwhile. Many of the sites can in fact be incorporated into a walk, being visited perhaps for a picnic and rest en route.

Most of the sites are owned by the large influential bodies of the area, i.e. National Trust and Lake District National Park, who also recognise the importance of opening up lakeside and riverside locations for the enjoyment of all. Most sites have actually been specifically designed for people's enjoyment next to water.

It is important to remember the owners who care for the sites and who are willing to allow public access, so always respect the sites and other visitors. Leaving litter and lighting fires are examples of behaviour that upsets the owners and other visitors and also damages the environment.

Safety is also an important aspect especially beside water and many of the hazards are described in the book, but it is up to individuals to ensure that their own safety is maintained.

Providing some care and consideration is taken, all the sites in the book can be very much enjoyed and spending a few hours relaxing by water is certainly a great way to appreciate the real beauty of the Lakes.

Site format

Within the book, each site has been considered under the following subheadings making it easier to ascertain if a site has particular attractions that you might desire.

- **Location**

A description of the exact location of the site relative to the body of water it adjoins.

- **Parking & facilities**

Giving details of the nearest public parking areas stating whether they are free or not. Also gives details of any facilities on or near the site e.g. toilets, food outlets, picnic tables and the nearest facilities if there are none at the site.

- **Access**

Details of pedestrian access from the parking area indicating how easy or difficult that may be.

- **Description**

A detailed description of the site itself including amount of space for spreading out and running around, outlook, access to the water and aspect/topography.

- **Sunshine & shelter**

A guide to the openness of the site i.e. how much sun can be expected throughout the day and how much shelter there is both from the sun and from any bad weather that might strike. The sunshine expectation is based on summer conditions so during Spring/Autumn there will tend to be less sun being lower in the sky through the day.

- **Beware**

A list of any site specific hazards e.g. dangerous unfenced roads or boats in the water.

- **Summary**

A summing up of the site and its attractions.

Site hazards

We all know about the enjoyment of spending a few hours by water, but it is important to be aware of the hazards involved.

All the sites in the book are beside water and the following points should be remembered when paddling, bathing or swimming.

- The rivers and lakes are all fed by water from the fells and even during hot weather the water is normally quite cold. Accidents due to people getting into difficulty in cold water do happen.

- Most the rivers and lakes of the area do benefit from having crystal clear water but deep water is sometimes not easily seen from the shore and care is always needed when paddling or bathing not to go out of one's depth.

The locations listed in the book are described in terms of suitability for activities based on the views of the author and current uses but the author cannot be held responsible for any injury or loss suffered at any of the sites.

All activities are undertaken at the discretion and risk of each individual.

The Lakes

The book describes permitted access around ten of the main lakes in the Lake District. There are a few more lakes than this, not to mention the numerous small tarns, but many of these are difficult to reach or have no public access or are not recommended for bathing. For example the Water Authority are not keen on people bathing in Thirlmere and Haweswater primarily because they are used to supply drinking water but they are also very deep and dangerous.

Although the lakes appear to change little it can be surprising how much the water level can alter between dry and wet periods. The lakes actually play quite a vital part in the landscape of the Lake District in that they naturally store rain water and help to control flooding of the area. One of the main reasons why the Lake District manages to cope with such a large amount of rainfall is that the lakes will absorb and store much of the rain and then it is released more slowly and flooding is not as severe.

Lake levels can vary quite significantly given substantial rainfall and this is often more pronounced in the summer when lakes can quickly go from being very low to very high. For example the level of Derwent Water has been known to rise by over a metre in less than 24 hours, which is an incredible amount of water when you consider the area of the lake.

These summer storms can make a significant difference to the shorelines and the subsequent rise in water levels will often submerge many of the beaches. In this respect the book will describe the sites during normal summer conditions but after a wet period there is a distinct possibility that the beaches described in the text may be under water and not accessible.

The book often refers to the 'beaches' that are found at the sites and it should be noted that these are not normally sandy beaches but tend to be made up of gravel or shingle. Nevertheless the beaches described still have much the same appeal as those found at the seaside and perhaps the only thing you might not be able to use is the traditional bucket and spade.

When describing the lakes the text will often refer to the HEAD or FOOT of the lake, or the view DOWN or UP the lake. To avoid any confusion, the end of the lake by the outflow is called the FOOT and the opposite end, normally by the main inflow, is called the HEAD. From anywhere around the lake, looking towards the outflow is looking DOWN the lake and looking away from the outflow is called looking UP the lake. The outflow is nearly always a single river but there are usually many inflows.

Bassenthwaite Lake

A popular quiz subject as it is actually the only 'lake' in the Lake District, the others are all 'waters' or 'meres'. The lake tends to be overlooked by people as they speed past on the busy A66 but it is a picturesque lake in a great setting guarded by the mighty Skiddaw. The lake is one of the largest being over 6km in length and is also the most northerly in Lakeland.

There are very few dwellings around the shores of the lake and the nearest good facilities are found some distance away at either Keswick or Cockermouth.

The lake has an ecologically sensitive shoreline where authorities are trying to conserve the natural environment and for this reason there is very little public lakeshore access around the lake apart from a couple of lovely sites along the western shore.

1. Bassenthwaite Lake at Hursthole Point and Blackstock Point.

Grid Reference NY219276 & NY222273. On the south-west shore of the lake adjacent to the main A66.

Parking & facilities

There is quite a large free car park on the opposite side of the A66 from Hursthole Point, which is accessed by turning onto the minor road signposted 'Thornthwaite' and driving 50m around the bend to the car park on the left, signposted 'Woodend Brow'.

Blackstock Point has a sizeable free lay-by parking area alongside the eastbound A66 carriageway. (Don't be fooled by the sign saying 'parking limited to 2 hrs', the applicable times are 9pm to 6am i.e. overnight!)

There are no facilities at either site, the nearest being in Keswick.

Access

Hursthole Point is only about 50m from the car park but there are some steep steps and the A66 must be crossed on the way.

Blackstock Point is reached directly from the lay-by via a stile over the fence, or there are easier gated entrances at either end of the lay-by.

Description

These two Points are real hidden gems. They are only about 400m apart and not surprisingly are very similar in appearance each forming a triangular headland jutting out into the lake. Both have wide grassy shorelines with great views especially across the lake towards Skiddaw, but also southwards towards Helvellyn and the hills surrounding Derwent Water, and northwards looking right down the lake.

Blackstock Point is the larger of the two but both have plenty of flat grassy areas on which to spread out with narrow shingle beaches providing good paddling and bathing access to the water. Both locations have trees set back from the water's edge which provide some shelter and are quite safe being protected from the road by fences.

Unfortunately there is an almost constant background hum from the nearby A66 but both sites remain quite unspoilt and largely undiscovered as people speed past, ignorant of the beautyspots they are passing.

Sunshine & shelter

The shorelines at both Points face either north or east across the lake and are quite open so sunshine can be expected throughout the day. The steep hills immediately to the west do mean that the sun will not last much into the evening. There are plenty of trees at each Point to provide shade and shelter.

Beware

- To get from the car park to the shore at Hursthole Point, the wide, busy and fast A66 must be crossed with its obvious dangers.

Summary

These two locations provide great access to the underrated Bassenthwaite Lake and the many attractions of both will provide a good time by the lake.

2. Bassenthwaite Lake at Ouse Bridge access area.

Grid Reference NY201320. At the northern end of the lake adjacent to the B5291 and Ouse Bridge.

Parking & facilities
There are two fairly large and free lay-by parking areas adjacent to the road about 50m apart.
There are no facilities on site, the nearest being in Cockermouth.

Access
From either car park there are fairly rough and steep paths with some steps down to the lakeshore which is only about 30m away. Some people may find access a little difficult.

Description
This lovely shore is at the northernmost tip of Bassenthwaite Lake near where the River Derwent pours out towards Cockermouth.
There is about 200m of shoreline access much of which is quite overgrown and wooded but providing the lake level is not too high there is a good length of shingle shore between the trees and the water.
At the southern end of this access area there are two separate secluded bays, about 30m apart, between the trees with shingle beaches and pleasant views across the lake.

To the north of this there is a much more open shingle beach which is quite wide and continues right round almost to Ouse Bridge itself.

There is very little grass along this shore and the shingle is quite coarse but if all you want to do is sit and relax then an enjoyable time can be had. Much of the shore has attractive views looking across and up the lake towards Skiddaw and the water is ideal for paddling or bathing. The shore is set below the road and is well shielded by the trees so the road does not impinge on the tranquillity of the site.

This is quite a peaceful location off the main beaten track and given the on-site parking it provides a good place to come and spend some time admiring one of the Lake District's more forgotten lakes.

Sunshine & shelter

The shore faces eastwards across the lake here and the shingle area will get a good deal of sun earlier in the day but the dense trees which back the shingle will tend to hide the sun completely from mid-afternoon onwards.

The trees will certainly provide plenty of shade and shelter throughout the day for those who need it.

Beware
- This part of Bassenthwaite is a conservation area and extra care should be taken not to destroy any vegetation or make any mess.
- There is no barrier between the shore and the road so children need to be careful.

Summary

These very pleasant beaches provide easy lakeshore access in a lovely tranquil setting but the lack of space may be a problem.

Buttermere

Small but perfectly formed, Buttermere is in a wonderful setting surrounded on three sides by high peaks and by Crummock Water immediately to the north-west. The narrow flat strip of land between the two lakes indicates that they were in fact one larger lake in ancient times but now each has its own identity. The high mountain range above the south-west shore dominates the landscape and includes some very impressive peaks including High Stile and Haystacks.

Buttermere village is only a few hundred metres from the lakeshore and is also picturesque so despite the remoteness of the area it does get quite busy in the summer.

There is a popular path around the lakeshore leading to some lovely shoreline access areas, which can be easily visited while walking around the lake.

3. Buttermere along the south-west shore.

Grid Reference NY174164 to NY183154. Sites along the south-west shore of the lake adjacent to Burtness Wood and the lakeshore path.

Parking & facilities
There is no parking close to the shore but it can be approached from either end of the lake. There are a number of car parking areas in Buttermere village giving access to the northern end of the lake, or there is a car park (fee payable) at Gatesgarth Farm (NY195150) giving access to the southern end of Burtness Wood.
There are no facilities along this shore, the nearest being in Buttermere village.

Access
There is a fairly good and mostly level path running from Buttermere village all along the south-west side of the lake and round to Gatesgarth Farm. There is a walk of about 600m from the village to the northern end of the lake, or 1.5km from Gatesgarth Farm to the southern end of Burtness Wood.

Description
The south-west shore of Buttermere is very beautiful and apart from the large number of people doing the popular round the lake walk, it is quite peaceful

being well away from any roads and the busy village of Buttermere. There is about 1.5km of lakeshore owned by the National Trust which has some very attractive shoreline access areas with excellent views across the lake to the surrounding fells. However, this side of the lake does tend to suffer from a lack of sun as the large trees of Burtness Wood which back the shoreline will soon shield the sun in the afternoon.

There are several good access areas along this shore which are described below in distance order if walking from Buttermere village:

The path from the village follows a track down to the lakeshore and at the point where you enter a field which runs along the shore (**NY174164**), there is about 100m of accessible shoreline adjacent to the river outflow from the lake. There is a narrow shingle beach area backed by a small stone retaining wall which protects the shoreline from the water and provides a nice sitting area. Immediately behind this is a large area of flat but quite rough grass under trees and some more open grass behind that. This shore is quite open with plenty of room to spread out and good access to the water and there are excellent views looking straight up the lake. The site will get plenty of sun throughout the day into the early evening before disappearing behind the high fells immediately to the west although the trees along the shore will provide shade and shelter if needs be. Being so handy to the village, this shore provides a great place to come and relax by the water in idyllic surroundings.

About 400m along the south-west shore from the footbridge over the river, there are some pleasant little shingle beaches adjacent to the footpath around the point where a small stream flows into the lake from the hills above (**NY176160**). The narrow shingle gives easy access to the water and along with the rough grass behind there is room to spread out with lovely views across the lake especially towards Grasmoor. The shore is backed and overhung by large trees which effectively hide the sun throughout the day so it is not a place for sun worshippers.

Immediately beyond this there is quite a length of wider shore with some rough grass and small areas of shingle which again have good access to the water and marvellous views but little afternoon sun.

About half way along the lake, around **NY180157**, there is a small bay with a fairly narrow shingle beach immediately adjacent to the path. There is a small stone retaining wall supporting the path which provides a pleasant place to relax and admire the view with perhaps a paddle and bathe in the lake. There is a lack of grass or space to spread out and the large trees behind will hide the sun most of the afternoon.

At this bay the path splits in two before meeting up again further on. Taking the shoreline path brings you to a lovely beach about 150m beyond the bay at **NY181157**. There is about 30m of shingle beach which is quite wide, providing a pleasant area to spread out although the path and trees are very close behind. This point protrudes out into the lake a little more than the previous beaches which gives it some spectacular views looking across and down the lake. The far end of this beach does have a small area of grass and a bench overlooking the lake where the views can be admired to the full. The trees are set a small distance back from the beach but they will still shield the sun from mid-afternoon onwards.

About 250m on again (**NY183154**) there is a gate where the footpath heads out of the trees and into the open and just before this gate there is another little shingle beach with some rough grass behind. There is room to spread out and the beach does give good paddling and bathing in the lake. The surrounding views over the lake are excellent but again there are overhanging trees which will hide the sun most of the afternoon.

Once out of the woods the shoreline is privately owned with no official access.

Sunshine & shelter
Details are given above but the shore tends to suffer from a lack of sun due to the many large trees and also the high steep slopes immediately to the west. There is certainly plenty of shade and shelter available with all the trees.

Summary
A very pleasant stretch of lakeshore where the beauty of the area can be enjoyed to the full although there is a distinct lack of afternoon sun and open areas.

4.   Buttermere along the north-east shore.

Grid Reference NY178165 to NY187156. Sites along the north-east shore of the lake adjacent to the lakeshore path.

Parking & facilities
Despite the fact that the road runs fairly close to the north-east shore, there is no parking or lakeshore access to these sites from the road and the shore must be approached along the footpath from either end of the lake.
There are a number of car parking areas in Buttermere village giving access to the northern end of the lake, or there is a car park (fee payable) at Gatesgarth Farm (NY195150) giving access to the southern end of the lake.
There are no facilities along this shore, the nearest being in Buttermere village.

Access
There is a fairly good path which is mostly level but a little rough in places running from Wilkinsyke Farm in Buttermere all along the north-east side of the lake which eventually joins the road and leads on to Gatesgarth Farm. The shortest route to a lakeshore access point is from Wilkinsyke Farm giving a walk of about 500m, or it is about 1km from Gatesgarth Farm to the first shoreline access point at that end of the lake.

Description

Despite being close to the road, the north-east side of Buttermere is still only accessible on foot and is quite peaceful with some lovely shoreline access areas where the lake can be fully enjoyed.

There tend to be more attractive beaches on this side of the lake than the other with some excellent views to the high mountains across the water and because the shore generally faces south-west there is also more sunshine on this side.

The best shore access areas are described below in distance order if walking from Buttermere village:

From Buttermere village, follow the footpath through Wilkinsyke Farm down to the lake where the shore access starts immediately and continues on along most of the shore.

From the point where the footpath meets the lake (**NY178165**), there are several hundred metres of quite narrow but very pleasant shingly areas giving access to the lake and some fine views. The land running down to the lake tends to be quite steep with the main path set slightly above the water so there is often a short rough unmade path leading down to the shoreline. There isn't a great deal of space to spread out but a relaxing time can be had next to the water. This shore has plenty of trees to provide shade and shelter but is quite open to the south-west so sunshine can be enjoyed throughout the day and well into the evening.

The land eventually levels out to an open field with rough grass and trees running along the shore around **NY183161**. There is a narrow shingle beach adjacent to this field giving access to the water and the grass along the water's edge provides some room to spread out. This shoreline has lovely open views across the lake and gets plenty of sunshine with some trees to provide shade and shelter. At the far end of this field is a larger shingle beach adjacent to the fence and through the gate is another good shingle beach where rowing boats are kept for hire. These rowing boats are owned by the National Trust and are available for hire through Mr & Mrs Parker at Dalegarth Farm, Tel: 017687 70233.

Immediately beyond this is the famous tunnel which has been hewn out of the solid rock and allows the footpath to remain level and close to the shore.

There is then about 250m of steep shoreline with no direct access to the water's edge until the start of an impressive beach at **NY186158**, adjacent to Hassnesshow Beck inflow. Here we find over 200m of quite wide and open beach made up of very small pieces of shingle with some trees dotted around. The beach curves right around the delta promontory of Hassnesshow Beck and has obviously been washed down from the hills above over many years. There is a small amount of grass with plenty of shingle where it is possible to spread out and enjoy the magnificent views both across the lake and up past the head of the lake towards the imposing valley of Warnscale.

South of this, as the path swings back towards the road, the shoreline is privately owned with no official access.

Sunshine & shelter

This entire shore tends to face south-west across the lake and is mostly quite open so sunshine can be expected throughout the day and well into the evening before dropping below the high slopes to the west.
There are also plenty of trees along the whole shore and shade or shelter is never far away.

Beware

- The lake bed around Hassnesshow Beck (NY186158) does shelve quite steeply away from the shore so care should be taken in the water.
- If walking from Gatesgarth Farm, there is quite a length of road walking with no path so beware of traffic.

Summary

A lovely lakeshore having a good range of shoreline access areas, all with excellent views and plenty of sun. A bit of a walk and there is never too much space but the lake can be enjoyed from any of the beaches described above.

Coniston Water

A popular lake for boating and scene of one of the most famous boating incidents in history - Donald Campbell's ill fated water world speed record attempt in 1967. The pace is now much more sedate with sailing being the main activity. The famous Gondola frequently steams around the lake and provides an excellent way of appreciating the area from the water.

The main centre is at Coniston village where there is a popular lakeshore access area at the boat launching site on Lake Road.

The other popular lakeshore access points are along the south-west shore which has some lovely sites but can get busy being adjacent to the main road.

There are also several very pleasant lakeshore access areas along the eastern shore which are much quieter, often with better views towards the Lakeland fells.

5.   Coniston Water at Lake Road car park & picnic site, Coniston.

Grid Reference SD308970. Lake Road runs from the centre of Coniston village about 1km down to the launch site on the lake.

Parking & facilities
There is a large free car park and the site also has a cafe plus toilets, picnic tables and some benches. Additional facilities can be found in nearby Coniston village.

Access
The lakeshore is immediately adjacent to the car park with a good level path leading to the beach and all the facilities.

Description
This is a very attractive site having a fair amount of flat open grass with picnic tables right next to a large gently shelving shingle beach.
The grassy picnic area is backed by trees and there is enough room to spread out but not really for running around as it can get quite crowded. There is more room on the wide shingle beach which is about 200m in length stretching northwards from the picnic tables around the small bay right up to the point where Yewdale Beck flows into the lake.

The main activity around this shore is boating and there are several jetties where many boats come and go including the lake launch and the Gondola. There are also boat launching facilities and boat hire at the site for those feeling a little more adventurous.

The main picnic area and beach are adjacent to the jetties and make a great location to relax, paddle and watch the boats as well as admire the pleasant views across the lake towards Grizedale Forest.

Because of the heavy boating activity it is advisable not to bathe or swim from the beach adjacent to the jetties as this could be dangerous. These activities are best undertaken on the southward facing beach adjacent to the beck inflow which is much quieter than the jetty area and has lovely views down the lake.

The site is handy to Coniston village and the free parking, flat grass and good beach make it a very desirable location.

Sunshine & shelter

The site faces south and east across the lake and is quite open so sunshine can be expected throughout the day. The picnic area will lose the sun in the early evening due to the trees immediately behind, but the beach will keep the sun a little longer before it disappears behind 'The Old Man of Coniston'.

As well as the trees at the picnic area there are numerous trees along the beach to provide shade and shelter.

Beware

- As this part of the lake is so popular for boating, take care if bathing.
- There is no barrier between the shore and the car park or road so children need to be careful.

Summary

An attractive site with excellent access and facilities and a lovely picnic area including a large expanse of good open shingle.

6.   Coniston Water at Brown Howe picnic site.

Grid Reference SD291911. On the western shore of the lake, just off the main A5084, approximately 3km south of Torver village.

Parking & facilities
There is a sizeable free car park at the site along with a toilet block and some benches.

Access
The car park is adjacent to and has easy access to the lakeshore. Water's edge is about 50m from the car park.

Description
This is an excellent lakeside location with almost everything you could wish for on a day out by the water. There is plenty of car parking, on site facilities, lots of lovely open grassy areas and great bathing in the lake, not to mention the magnificent views up the lake towards the main Lakeland fells.
There is approximately 200m of accessible lakeshore which has formed into several small but picturesque beaches with large trees lined along the back edge. The water's edge is shingly and gives good access to the water for paddling and

bathing. Behind the shingle and trees there is a substantial amount of gently sloping grass which can get quite crowded but provides plenty of open space to spread out and run around.

Because of the trees along the shore there isn't a great view from the grass but by moving down to the water's edge, excellent views can be had towards the head of the lake and the mountains beyond.

Sunshine & shelter
The lakeshore faces eastwards across the lake and there are plenty of open areas where sunshine can be had throughout the day. The large trees which shield the site from the road will also shield the sun completely in the early evening.

There are plenty of trees around the site providing shade and shelter.

Beware
● The site is directly fenced from the main road but not from the car park.

Summary
A superb picturesque lakeside location with plenty of good open spaces and great bathing making for an ideal day out by the lake.

7.   Coniston Water at Blawith Common.

Grid Reference SD289904. On the western shore of the lake, off the main A5084, about 2km north from the hamlet of Blawith.

Parking & facilities
There are three separate free parking areas along the roadside here, where the unfenced road runs across Blawith Common. All three give access to the shore. There are no facilities at the site, the nearest being in Coniston village, although toilets can be found at the nearby Brown Howe access area.

Access
There are paths running from each of the parking areas down to the lakeshore. The most northerly car park at SD287904 gives easiest access to the shore with a fairly level path providing about 200m easy walk. The paths from the other two parking areas are rougher, more hilly and longer.

Description
This is an idyllic location with several lovely little cove-like beaches and plenty of good open flat grass. The site is at the southern end of the lake and is a real hidden gem being quite secluded and well away from the road.

There is a path which joins the three parking areas which also goes some distance along the shore but the best place to locate is on the promontory at the northern end of the site. This promontory has several small idyllic 'coves' with shingle beaches and there is also a fair amount of flat grass where you can spread out and run around overlooking the lake. All the beaches provide excellent access to the water for paddling and bathing.

The aspect is mostly southwards towards the foot of the lake and there are attractive open views down the remainder of the lake to the point where it pours into the River Crake.

Blawith Common provides a great place to explore and there are plenty of good paths in the area, especially the one across the road to Beacon Tarn which makes a pleasant little walk being only about 1km over the hill from the road.

Sunshine & shelter

The beaches generally face south and east and are quite open so will get the sun throughout the day. The promontory does have a number of trees around it and the larger ones to the west will tend to hide the sun in the early evening. More sun can be had on the south-facing shore, nearer to the car park, which is more open to the west.

The trees around the site will provide plenty of shade and shelter.

Beware

- Although the site is some distance from the road there is no barrier between the two.
- The lake is narrow at this point and is quite popular with boats so take care if bathing.

Summary

A real hidden gem of a site with some good grassy areas and lovely beaches, quite secluded but still easily accessible.

8.   Coniston Water at Low Peel Near & High Peel Near.

Grid Reference SD296914 to SD296918. On the eastern shore of the lake about 2km north from the hamlet of High Nibthwaite.

Parking & facilities

There is some roadside parking adjacent to the site for a small number of cars only and care should be taken not to obstruct the road. Otherwise there is further free parking at Selside Beck car park (SD296909) about 500m south of Low Peel Near, or Rigg Wood car park (SD299923) about 600m north of High Peel Near.

There are no facilities on site, the nearest being in Coniston village.

Access

From the road that runs alongside the site there are several paths leading down to the lakeshore. The distance to the shore from the road varies from nothing at Low Peel Near to about 200m at High Peel Near. Paths can be a little rough but are basically flat and easy.

Description

This is quite a large area of National Trust access land with almost 1km of continuous shoreline which is considered as one site here.

The area is mostly wooded with much of the shore consisting of rocky outcrops or overgrown areas but there are several good shingle beaches where an enjoyable time can be had by the lake.

The site is normally quite peaceful, being on the quiet side of the lake and is mostly well away from the road anyway.

The best beach is the one next to the road at Low Peel Near which is very open with attractive views to the south and great paddling or bathing in the lake. The other beaches tend to be a bit more enclosed and shadowed by trees but still provide excellent sites to enjoy the lake. Though quite small the beaches all provide enough room to spread out and there is good playing and exploring along the shoreline and in the woods behind. The only decent grassy area is behind the beach at Low Peel Near and this has plenty of room to spread out and run around.

The lovely Peel Island provides great exploring and is only about 100m offshore from High Peel Near so can easily be reached with a small boat.

Sunshine & shelter

Most of the beaches face south or west across the lake and sun can be expected throughout the day. There are low hills to the west which will eventually hide the sun but not until late evening.

The number of trees does mean that much of the area is kept in shade through the day although a sunny spot can always be found, especially around Low Peel Near, and there is certainly plenty of shade and shelter.

Beware
- The road runs quite close to the shore and although there is a wall between the two, there are plenty of open gaps so children need to be careful.
- If parking at either of the two car parks away from the site, there is quite a length of road walking involved with its obvious dangers.

Summary

An excellent wooded lakeside area which has some great little beaches in peaceful locations.

9. Coniston Water along the eastern shore, north of Peel Island.

The eastern shore has several small access areas along the stretch between Peel Island and the northern end of the lake as listed below:

- Rigg Wood car park & picnic area - SD299923
- Dodgson Wood car park - SD299928
- Bailiff Wood car park - SD303935
- Machell's Coppice car park & picnic area - SD310952
- Monk Coniston car park - SD316978

Shore at Monk Coniston

Parking & facilities
- Rigg Wood car park & picnic area - free car park and picnic tables only.
- Dodgson Wood car park - free car park only.
- Bailiff Wood car park - free car park only.
- Machell's Coppice car park & picnic area - free car park, picnic tables and toilets.
- Monk Coniston car park - Pay & Display car park, benches and toilets.

The nearest main facilities to these sites can be found in Coniston village.

Access
In all cases the car parks are located adjacent to the lakeshore allowing relatively easy access.

Description
The eastern shore of Coniston Water has several car parking areas along its length, each allowing quite easy access to the lakeshore. At each location the lakeshore tends to be made up of narrow shingle with plenty of trees so conditions are not great for a full day by the lake. Because there is only limited potential at each location and they are all similar in nature, they have been grouped together here but there are certainly sufficient attractions to enjoy spending some time by the lake.

- At Rigg Wood the car park & picnic area are set slightly back from the lake under trees and there are several picnic tables in a pleasant woodland setting with glimpses of the lake. Across the road the lakeshore can easily be accessed and provides some small areas of shingle and a little headland backed by trees with lovely views across the lake. The jetty here is the point where the lake launch stops on the eastern shore so a boat ride can also be incorporated into the day.
- Dodgson Wood car park is also across the road from the lake and the lakeshore access consists of about 200m of narrow shingle with trees behind giving open views across the lake towards the mountains beyond.
- Bailiff Wood car park is again set back from the lake and there is some narrow shingle lakeshore which is accessed by short but quite steep and rough paths. There are a lot of trees along the shore and little room to spread out although the views are again good across the lake. About 100m south of the car park is 'The Cabin' bay which does have a more open shingle beach with good views down the lake.
- Machell's Coppice has a large car park & picnic area set back from the lake under trees. The shore is a level walk across the road and has about 150m of open shingle which is quite wide in places backed by trees. This shore mostly has a south-west aspect with open views down the lake. There are also forest walks from the site.
- Monk Coniston car park gives access to a lovely shoreline which has two distinct parts. At the head of the lake, adjacent to the road, is about 100m of quite wide and open fine shingle backed by trees and some benches giving attractive views right down the lake. Alternatively, between the car park and the launch jetty, adjacent to the footpath, there are a series of narrow shingle beaches between trees which provide more shelter than at the head of the lake and look straight across the water towards 'The Old Man of Coniston'. A trip on the lake launch is also an option here.

Sunshine & shelter
The shoreline generally faces in a westerly direction across the lake and sunshine can be had throughout the day. All shorelines do have plenty of trees close behind which can hide the sun from certain sections at certain times but sunshine can always be easily found. The picnic sites and car parks are always set amongst trees where there will be no sun but the shore is never far away. Sun should last well into the evening before eventually dipping behind the Coniston mountain range away to the west.
There are certainly plenty of trees to provide shade and shelter at all sites.

Beware
- At all sites the road is unfenced and apart from at Monk Coniston, it does have to be crossed to reach the shore, so although the road is mostly quiet some caution is needed.

Summary
A good choice of tranquil lakeshore access points offering easy access from the car with some lovely shingle and views but limited opportunity for spreading out and spending a full day.

Shore at Machell's Coppice

Crummock Water

Closely related to Buttermere, Crummock Water is substantially larger and more varied than its partner. The surrounding land is quite flat and open at each end with Buttermere lake close to the southern end and Lorton Vale extending northwards from the northern end where the River Cocker pours out towards Cockermouth. Along each side of the lake are some impressive mountains with Grasmoor, Mellbreak and Red Pike all very prominent.

As with Buttermere the nearest centre is Buttermere village which is directly between the two lakes and can get overcrowded during the summer.

Crummock Water itself can get relatively busy along its eastern shore as there are several locations where there is parking near the lake with good lakeshore access. The western shore is much more remote but still has some great lakeshore access areas where the tranquillity and spectacular views can be better enjoyed.

10.   Crummock Water by Mill Beck inflow.

Grid Reference NY167173. At the head of the lake, about 800m west of Buttermere village.

Parking & facilities
There are a couple of large Pay & Display car parks in Buttermere village and the one behind the Fish Hotel next to Mill Beck is the most handy for this site. Alternatively, there is a free lay-by parking area on the B5289 about 1km north-west of Buttermere village at the point where the road meets the lake.
There are plenty of facilities in Buttermere village but none on site.

Access
From the Mill Beck car park in Buttermere there is a good level path which follows the southern bank of Mill Beck and leads directly to the shore of Buttermere, a walk of about 1km.
From the lay-by on the B5289 there is a path, which is quite rough and steep in places, that follows the lakeshore around to the Mill Beck inflow, a walk of about 500m.

Description
This is a beautiful and tranquil shoreline nicely hidden away from the often busy village of Buttermere, where it is possible to spend an idyllic few hours enjoyment by the lake.

There is an excellent fine shingle beach with lovely views down the lake and there is also some good flat grass with plenty of room to spread out. The shoreline is about 200m long with Mill Beck entering the lake about half way along. The lake provides great bathing and the beck also presents an ideal paddling and play area being normally quite shallow and slow as it enters the lake.

To the south of the beck, adjacent to the wooded rocky knoll, the beach is wide with some grass behind although there are numerous trees dotted around on both the grass and the shingle.

Around the beck inflow and to the north of it, the beach is still wide but much more open with a few gorse bushes and there is some open flat grass behind the beach.

At the far northern end of the site, where the path leads on into the trees, are some rowing boats which are owned by the National Trust and are available for hire through Mr & Mrs McKenzie at Wood House, Tel: 017687 70208.

The fact that the site is set well away from any roads or hazards does mean it can be enjoyed not only in peace but also in safety.

The near perfect beach dotted with trees in such an idyllic setting certainly gives the shore a touch of paradise and despite the walk from the parking areas, the reward is good justification for the trip.

Sunshine & shelter
The shoreline faces north and west here with plenty of open space so sunshine can be expected throughout the day. High fells across the lake to the west will eventually hide the sun later in the evening.

There is plenty of shade and shelter around the trees to the south of the beck.

Summary
A near perfect lakeside setting which is very picturesque with lovely views and magnificent shingle beaches.

11. Crummock Water at Rannerdale.

Grid Reference NY162183. On the eastern shore of the lake, adjacent to the main B5289, about 2km north-west of Buttermere village.

Parking & facilities
There is a small but free car park on the opposite side of the road to the lake at NY163184, or a small free lay-by next to the road at NY162183.
There are no facilities on site, the nearest being in Buttermere village.

Access
From the larger car park there is an easy flat walk about 50m along the road, followed by a rough path which is only a few metres down to the shore.
The lay-by is directly above and adjacent to the shore.

Description
This is a very small lakeshore access area which despite its size does have some redeeming features.
The shingle beach is about 50m long but only a few feet wide with an almost vertical slope behind to the road above. There is room to sit with good access to the shallow water for paddling and bathing but there is certainly no room to run

around. The beach is quite open with lovely views across the lake towards Mellbreak.

At the southern end of the beach is quite a large rock formation with some small areas of grass, which juts out into the lake and provides a great place to sit and admire the views from beside the road.

The lack of space means it is probably not a place to spend any length of time and the adjacent unfenced road is an obvious hazard to children.

However, with such easy access from the road and some attractive open views down the lake it makes a pleasant place to relax by the water.

Sunshine & shelter

The shore here faces north and west down the lake and is very open so sunshine can be expected throughout the day. The steep high slopes of Mellbreak across the lake to the west will eventually hide the sun later in the evening.

There are no trees to provide any shade or shelter though the steep slope behind the beach will often provide some shelter from the wind.

Beware

- Very deep water adjacent to the rocks.
- The road has no footpath or fence next to the shore and can be busy and dangerous.

Summary

A pleasant but very small shoreline area with easy access and a lovely little beach providing good paddling and bathing in the lake.

12.   Crummock Water at Low Ling Crag.

Grid Reference NY157183. Midway along the western shore of the lake.

Parking & facilities
The nearest parking is at the Pay & Display car park behind the Fish Hotel, adjacent to Mill Beck in Buttermere village.
There are no facilities on site, the nearest being in Buttermere village.

Access
From the car park, walk back around the Fish Hotel to the bridleway which leads to Buttermere lake and Crummock Water. The Crummock Water path splits right after a couple of hundred metres, then continues across the river and turns right towards the lake. Continue to follow the lakeshore path until Low Ling Crag is reached.
Total walking distance is about 3km each way on quite rough but fairly level paths.

Description
Low Ling Crag is a fascinating little headland which protrudes unexpectedly from the western shore of Crummock Water about 80m into the lake. The crag

itself is right at the end of the headland and is not really a 'crag' as its rocky and grassy slopes rise quite gently out of the water to a height of only a few metres. The main feature of the site is the causeway-like beach that joins the crag to the mainland. Either side of the causeway feature are wide and open sweeping shingle beaches, one facing southwards with exceptional views towards the head of the lake and the high fells beyond, and the other facing northwards with good open views down the lake. The two beaches are separated by quite a wide strip of open flat grass and when combined with the shingle there is certainly plenty of room to spread out with easy access to the water for paddling and bathing.

Part of the attraction with two opposite facing beaches so close together is that you can 'pick-a-view', so for example if you get bored of looking up the lake you can switch and look down the lake.

The only drawback is the 6km round walk from Buttermere village but it is a very pleasant walk which presents no real problems for able-bodied people and the reward of the great shoreline at the end makes the trip well worthwhile.

Sunshine & shelter
Both beaches are very open and sunshine can be expected throughout the day but the steep, high slopes of Mellbreak immediately to the west ensure it will not last into the evening.

There are a few small gorse bushes but very little shade or shelter and being so exposed and isolated the weather is certainly an important consideration.

Summary
A lovely little headland which provides exceptional beaches and views although a lengthy walk is involved.

13.   Crummock Water around Lanthwaite Wood.

Grid Reference NY152208 & NY149200. Sites around the northern end of the lake.

Parking & facilities
There is a large Pay & Display car park at Lanthwaite Wood, adjacent to Scalehill Bridge (NY149215) (free for National Trust members).
There are no facilities on site, the nearest being in Cockermouth.

Access
From the car park, a good and fairly level track leads about 700m through the woods to the lakeshore. A good but slightly rougher path leads on to the site along the western shore.

Description
The northern end of Crummock Water is very picturesque and has a couple of excellent lakeshore access points with great beaches and fantastic views, either up the lake towards the High Stile mountain range or across the lake towards Grasmoor. The sites are a little walk from the car park but you are more than rewarded with tranquil and safe settings in idyllic locations.

The two different sites are described as follows:

41

- Foot of lake adjacent to River Cocker outflow, NY152208.

At the point where the track from the car park meets the lake there is a delightful shingle beach which is quite small but in a lovely setting with splendid views straight up the lake. The shingle area is only about 30m long but is quite wide and open with plenty of surrounding trees. There is room to spread out but not enough to run around and there are also a couple of benches to sit and admire the views. Paddling is possible in the shallow water but due to the proximity of the Water Authority weir, swimming is prohibited. The beach faces southwards up the lake and is quite open so sunshine can be expected throughout the day. The surrounding trees provide shade and shelter but will tend to shield the sun completely in the early evening.

- Western shore at bay beyond headland, NY149200.

From the point where the car park track meets the lake, an additional walk of about 800m along the western shore path takes you around a headland and into a superb curving bay which probably has one of the finest settings and beaches in the whole area.

There is a wide open shingle beach, which is about 200m in length, curving gloriously around the bay. The beach faces south and east up the lake with magnificent views towards the head of the lake and the surrounding fells and there is plenty of shallow water making it ideal for paddling and bathing.

The beach gives plenty of room to spread out and there is also a small amount of flat grass behind with a few small trees and bushes to provide some shade and shelter. Despite the lower slopes of Mellbreak to the west, sunshine should last well into the evening.

The whole site is very secluded, well away from any roads and slightly off the beaten track which helps to enhance the feeling of beauty and if there is such a thing as lakeside Utopia then this site certainly comes close.

Sunshine & shelter

Details are given above.

Beware

- At the point where the River Cocker flows out of the lake towards Cockermouth there is a Water Authority structure which enables local drinking water to be taken out of the lake and for this reason the structure is very much out of bounds and swimming is forbidden.

Summary

Two varied lakeside access areas which are both very picturesque and peaceful with some lovely beaches and views providing ideal settings to enjoy the lake. A bit of a walk is involved but the sites certainly make it worthwhile.

Derwent Water

Affectionately called 'the Queen of the Lakes' it is certainly a majestic lake in a fantastic position. Wherever you look there are superb sights with Skiddaw, Cat Bells, Borrowdale and Lodore Falls being just some of them.

There are many lakeshore access areas, with most of the shore apart from the north-west side having public access.

The popular shore is the eastern side mainly because the Borrowdale road runs alongside making access easy and there are also some very good sites close to Keswick itself.

The western shore is much more peaceful with a lovely footpath running along its length but no road anywhere near. There are some great access areas south of Hawse End which can still quite easily be reached by catching the lake launch which frequently runs from Keswick and calls at three different locations along the western shore.

The main centre is Keswick which is also probably the most popular place in the Lakes.

14. Derwent Water on the western shore between Hawse End jetty and the southern end of the lake.

Grid Reference NY251213 to NY256190.

Hawse End jetty

Parking & facilities

There is only one notable car park which is close to the western shore and that is near Hawse End at NY247212. This car park is quite small but free and consists of some small areas of rough ground under the trees adjacent to the road.

There are no facilities along the western shore apart from the odd picnic table and bench, the nearest facilities being in Keswick.

Access

From the car park near Hawse End, a rough path leads quite steeply downhill for about 300m to the lake and Hawse End jetty.

The best method of accessing this shore is to board one of the lake launches which frequently run from Keswick in both directions around the lake. There are three separate landing jetties along the western shore and by using the launch the car can be left at Keswick and an enjoyable boat ride can be had as well.

The lakeshore path is slightly rough but mostly good and level although there are often short rough unmade paths leading down to the shoreline.

Description

The western shore of Derwent Water is very beautiful and tranquil but quite remote with the lakeshore footpath being the only way of travel along the shore. There is about 2km of the western shore which has public access and this description takes us from Hawse End jetty (NY251213) down to the southern end of the lake (NY256190) describing the best shorelines along the way.

Around **Hawse End jetty (NY251213)** there is an attractive shingle beach with trees dotted around and fine views across the lake.

To the south of the jetty there is quite a length of beach which is fairly wide with hard shingle and stone providing access to the water. There is some grass behind and when combined with the shingle, there is plenty of room to spread out with some trees along the grass.

At the head of **Otterbield Bay (NY252209)** there is a section of fenced-off shore, but on the south-east side of the bay, alongside the little headland, is a wide and open fine shingle beach which has some open flat grass adjacent to it. The site faces north and west and has excellent views down the lake towards Skiddaw. The area is mostly open so will get plenty of sun although parts of the beach are somewhat overshadowed by a few large trees which will provide shade and shelter.

The shore around Hawse End and Otterbield Bay has some areas that are quite open to the west and should keep the sun later into the evening.

From the headland at Otterbield Bay down to **Low Brandelhow jetty (NY252207)** there is quite a length of fairly narrow and rough stony shoreline with some rough grass behind which still has lovely views but limited space.

South of the jetty the shore is fairly wide with shingle/stone but not much in the way of grass.

At the head of **Victoria Bay (NY253206)** is a fine curving beach with great views northwards down the lake towards Skiddaw but unfortunately the dense overhanging trees will mean there is little sun throughout the day.

Withesike Bay (NY252203) again has some quite wide shingle/stone beaches with attractive views across the lake and good bathing. At the southern end of the bay there is a solitary picnic table next to the footpath.

There are fairly narrow beaches most the way from Withesike Bay heading south to **High Brandelhow jetty (NY252198)** and although they provide good lake access and views, there is not a great deal of space and the shore tends to be quite stony.

Adjacent to High Brandelhow jetty itself there are a couple of nicely positioned picnic tables under the trees and a wide shingle/stone beach with fine views across the lake.

About 100m south of the jetty, around into **Brandelhow Bay (NY252196)**, there is a wide and open shingle/stone shore with a high scree bank directly behind. This beach is more open than many on this side of the lake so more sunshine can be expected and the views are again good.

The peninsula with the house between Brandelhow Bay and **Abbot's Bay (NY253195)** is privately owned with no shore access.

It is well worth walking along the wooded headland between Abbot's Bay and **Myrtle Bay (NY254193)** where some lovely little beaches can be found. This shoreline is a bit more rough and rocky than that further north but there are a number of often quite secluded little shingle beaches, many with superb views down the lake towards Keswick and Skiddaw. The tip of the headland has a bench where the views can be fully enjoyed.

This section of the shore makes for good exploring with its inlets and protrusions and there are some great places to relax and admire the views as well as paddle or bathe in the lake.

Myrtle Bay has a few picturesque beaches dotted around it, but again they are quite small with little open space to run around. The headland to the south of Myrtle Bay also has a fantastic viewpoint at its tip with a well positioned bench and probably one of the best views in the area.

Sunshine & shelter

Most of the bays and beaches on this side of the lake face east and north but unless otherwise stated, there are usually large trees directly behind the shore so although sun can be found near the water's edge, there is plenty of shade behind. The sun will often completely disappear behind the trees in the late afternoon although some of the more open areas will keep the sun longer.

Even if trees can be avoided, the steep slopes of Cat Bells immediately to the west mean that the sun will not last much into the evening.

Beware
- If bathing near to the jetties, watch out for the frequently running lake launches.

Summary

The remoteness of the western shore of Derwent Water does mean it is very tranquil away from the main hustle and bustle around Keswick. The shore described above is basically one long beach with literally dozens of more obvious attractive beaches, many of which have idyllic settings and excellent views across and down the lake. The beaches tend to be fairly small and stony with plenty of trees around but they provide great places to relax and take in the atmosphere of the area in peace.

15.   Derwent Water from Barrow Bay to Kettlewell.

Grid Reference NY269204 to NY267195. On the eastern shore of the lake, about 3km south of Keswick.

Kettlewell

Parking & facilities
There is a fairly small Pay & Display car park at Kettlewell (NY267195) (free for National Trust members), and there is also a small free car park just up the Watendlath road at NY269203, which is closest to Barrow Bay.
There are no facilities on site, the nearest being in Keswick.

Access
Barrow Bay can be accessed directly from the Watendlath road car park although there are some steep steps to negotiate.
Kettlewell car park gives direct and level shore access.
The large expanse of shore access which juts out into the lake around Barrow Beck can be accessed from either car park along quite rough but level paths, giving a maximum walking distance of about 500m.
Alternatively, take the Derwent Water launch from Keswick to Ashness Gate jetty which is in Barrow Bay.

Description
This stretch of shoreline is about 1km long and has three distinct shore access areas which are described below in order from north to south:

47

- Barrow Bay (NY269204 to NY267202).

The bay sweeps around in a west and north facing arc from the landing jetty at Ashness Gate, round to the point where Barrow Beck spills into the lake. The shore is made up of wide and open but quite rough stone/shingle beaches with some trees behind and excellent views across and down the lake towards the mountains beyond. There is good paddling and bathing but no grass to speak of and space is fairly limited with little room to run around.

- Barrow Beck delta (NY267202 to NY267197).

This delta protrudes into Derwent Water either side of Barrow Beck, which tumbles into the lake from the hills immediately to the east having recently passed under the famous Ashness Bridge. South of Barrow Beck there is a very wide and open shingle/stone shore with grass behind, all of which is quite rough. Not a perfect surface but there is plenty of room to spread out and run around with good lake access and because the shore protrudes into the lake there are superb views in all directions including Borrowdale, Skiddaw and across to Cat Bells. This stretch is set away from the road so the tranquillity of the area can be fully enjoyed. The shore continues like this with the odd tree for about 400m to the point where it rejoins the road.

- Kettlewell car park (NY267195).

This Pay & Display car park gives direct access to about 60m of wide and open but quite rough stony shore with no grass and plenty of trees behind. There is normally quite a lot of exposed beach on which to spread out, which provides easy access to the lake for paddling and bathing. Despite the lack of good space this is a very pleasant position to come and enjoy the lake with some lovely views across the water to the mountains beyond.

Sunshine & shelter

The shore along this stretch of the lake generally faces westwards across the water and there are plenty of open spaces where sunshine can be enjoyed throughout the day. High mountains to the west are far enough away to mean that the sun will last nearly all evening.

There are numerous trees dotted around to provide shade and shelter.

Beware
- Both Barrow Bay and Kettlewell car park have direct open access to the road so care needs to be taken with children.
- If parking at the Watendlath road car park, the main road must be crossed and it can be quite busy and fast.

- If bathing around Ashness Gate jetty watch out for the lake launches which land at the jetty fairly frequently.

Summary

This stretch of shoreline is quite contrasting but generally provides easy access with some lovely open but quite rough beaches. The aspect of this shore gives excellent views across the lake with plenty of sunshine as well. A good place to spend a few hours enjoying the lake.

Barrow Beck delta

16.   Derwent Water around Calfclose Bay.

Grid Reference NY267218 to NY269209. On the eastern shore of the lake adjacent to the Borrowdale road, about 2km south of Keswick.

Parking & facilities
There is a large National Trust Pay & Display car park at Great Wood on the opposite side of the road from Calfclose Bay (free for National Trust members). There are no facilities on site, the nearest being in Keswick.

Access
From the car park, head back to the main road from where there are various paths leading through the wall about 100m to the shore at Calfclose Bay. Paths are fairly good but a little rough in places as are those leading northwards and southwards from the bay.
If coming from Keswick, there is a bus which stops right next to the bay.

Description
Calfclose Bay provides a wonderful shore access area with plenty of good shingle/stone beaches and marvellous views across the lake towards the surrounding high mountains.

There are basically three parts to this access area. Firstly is Calfclose Bay itself, secondly is around the headland just to the north of the bay where there is more shoreline access overlooking Lord's Island and thirdly is to the south of the bay where there is further shore access.

The picturesque Calfclose Bay swings around in a big arc over a distance of about 500m and although there are plenty of wide open beaches, there are no real grassy areas with little room to run around. The beaches give good paddling and bathing but are a little rough with plenty of stone mixed with the shingle and there are trees all along the back of the shore. The southern section of the bay has lovely views across the lake towards Grisedale Pike and Crag Hill, whereas the northern section gives great views up the lake towards Borrowdale. The headland at the northern end of the bay has a bench giving fantastic views of the lake and surrounding fells.

Around the headland to the north of the bay is about 200m of lakeshore access in the form of a wide shingle/stone shore with some patchy grass behind and a few trees dotted around behind that. The shore is still quite rough but again has excellent views across the lake and tends to be a bit more peaceful than Calfclose Bay itself.

To the south of Calfclose Bay, the wide shingle/stone shore continues for about 200m and because this shore is a bit more open and exposed than in the bay, the views are more spectacular in all directions including Borrowdale and Skiddaw. There is some rough grass at the back of the shore with trees behind that. As the shore continues southwards it swings back towards the road where there is a lovely beach (NY269209), which is about 100m long with wide shingle/stone and trees dotted along the back. From here there are great views over the lake and straight up Borrowdale.

Sunshine & shelter
The shore generally faces westwards across the lake and although there are a number of trees, they are set back from the shoreline so sunshine can be expected throughout the day. High mountains to the west are far enough away to mean that the sun will last nearly all evening.

The trees behind the shore do provide plenty of shade and shelter if needs be.

Beware
- When crossing the road from the car park to the shore, visibility isn't great and traffic can appear quickly and suddenly. There is a wall between the road and the shore with open gaps for access.

Summary
A very picturesque shore with easy access, great views and plenty of open beaches but there is a lack of good space to spread out and run around with quite a rough shingle/stone surface.

17.   Derwent Water from Friar's Crag to Strandshag Bay.

Grid Reference NY264223 to NY266221. On the north-east shore of the lake about 600m south from the 'Theatre by the Lake' in Keswick.

Parking & facilities
The nearest parking is the large Pay & Display car park adjacent to the 'Theatre by the Lake' in Keswick.
There are no facilities on site but toilets and food kiosks can be found near to the boat jetties and the Theatre.

Access
From the Theatre car park, walk towards the lake to the boat jetties, then continue onwards towards Friar's Crag. Bypass the crag to reach the shore to the east of the crag. Paths are all good and fairly level and the first shore access point is about 600m from the car park.

Description
This is a magnificent shoreline access area with a lovely shingle shore and plenty of flat open grass behind on which to spread out and run around.
The only way to access this site is by walking the short distance from Keswick

but you are rewarded with a very picturesque area which is far enough away from the busy town to get some peace and tranquillity and enjoy the lake.

Between Friar's Crag and Strandshag Bay there is about 300m of open lakeshore which provides excellent access to the lake for paddling and bathing. The grass and shingle shore is very wide and behind that is the footpath with some trees running alongside. When the level of the lake is low, the beach adjacent to Friar's Crag forms an interesting little water inlet feature which is nice and safe for playing in. With all the wide open spaces and the lack of roads or any other hazards this site is certainly family friendly.

The views all along this shore are spectacular both across the lake towards Grisedale Pike, Crag Hill and Cat Bells and also up the lake towards Borrowdale with Lord's Island in the foreground. The adjacent Friar's Crag is famous for its spectacular setting and views but does get quite crowded so to relax on this shore and enjoy the same impressive scenery is certainly a very appealing option.

Considering how good this site is and its closeness to Keswick, it is surprising that it remains relatively quiet but it is certainly well worth the trip to spend some time enjoying the real beauty of Derwent Water.

Sunshine & shelter
The shore faces south and west across the lake and is mostly open so sunshine can be expected throughout the day. High mountains to the west are far enough away to mean that the sun will last nearly all evening.

There are some trees dotted along the back of the shoreline which provide shade and shelter.

Summary
An idyllic site in a great setting being very picturesque and tranquil with plenty of good open space and still within easy walking distance of Keswick.

18.   Derwent Water at Crow Park in Keswick.

Grid Reference NY263229. At the northern end of the lake adjacent to the boat jetties and the 'Theatre by the Lake' in Keswick.

Parking & facilities
The nearest car park is the large Pay & Display adjacent to the 'Theatre by the Lake' in Keswick. There are also several car parks nearby in Keswick itself. There are no facilities on the site itself but toilets and food kiosks can be found near to the boat jetties.

Access
From the Theatre car park, Crow Park is directly across the road from the Theatre entrance. There is a good path which leads about 100m gently down to the lakeshore.
If coming from the centre of Keswick simply follow the directions to the Theatre which is about 500m from the town centre.

Description
Crow Park has long been a popular recreational site for the people of Keswick and justifiably so with its huge expanse of good open grass and lovely beach

area, not to mention the fabulous views which are arguably the best of any lakeshore site in the Lakes.

The shingle beach is about 80m long and provides great access to the lake for paddling and bathing. Behind the beach the grass slopes gently up providing an excellent position to spread out, run around or relax with fantastic views over the lake towards the many impressive surrounding hills and also of the nearby boat jetties with their frequent boat movements. A site that can boast commanding views of Derwent Water, Derwent Isle, Borrowdale, Cat Bells and Crag Hill is bound to be impressive.

The lake launch frequently departs from the jetties travelling around the lake and this makes a good trip, or if you prefer there are rowing and motor boats for hire. The fact that the site is so handy to Keswick does mean it can be busy but there is plenty of space and a great time can be had with activities to suit everyone.

Sunshine & shelter

The park and beach face south and west up the lake and are very open so sunshine can be expected throughout the day. High mountains to the west are far enough away to mean that the sun will last nearly all evening.

There is no shade or shelter to speak of in the park with no trees near to the shore.

Beware

● If bathing beware of the many boats which use this part of the lake.

Summary

A fantastic site, very handy for Keswick with acres of good open grass and excellent views of the lake and mountains beyond.

Grasmere

In the heart of the Lakes and Wordsworth territory, Grasmere lake is justifiably popular in its spectacular setting surrounded by high fells and next to the picturesque but busy village of Grasmere. Unfortunately, the busy A591 runs along the eastern shore and rather spoils that side of the lake but it is possible to get away from the hustle and bustle on the southern and western sides where there is a pleasant footpath along the shore.

The only good shoreline access area is at the southern end of the lake adjacent to the outlet of the River Rothay where it heads off towards nearby Rydal Water. Here there is a lovely beach and shore area, but anyone thinking of bathing should note that Grasmere does have some problems with pollution in the lake and this activity is not always recommended.

19.   Grasmere.

Grid Reference NY343059. At the southern end of Grasmere adjacent to the River Rothay outlet.

Parking & facilities
There are a couple of large National Trust Pay & Display car parks either side of the main road at White Moss Common between Grasmere and Rydal, around NY350065 (free to National Trust members).
Toilets are provided by the car parks but there are no facilities on site, the nearest being in Grasmere village.

Access
From the car parks there is a good but slightly rough and undulating path which leads south and west about 800m to the shore of Grasmere. This shouldn't present any difficulties to able-bodied people.

Description
This is a very picturesque lakeshore access area with a lovely beach providing excellent views across Grasmere to the surrounding fells which really do surround the lake here.

There is about 70m of wide and open shingle beach providing some room to spread out with easy access to the lake for paddling and bathing. Behind the beach there is a narrow area of grass to sit on but behind that the ground slopes quite steeply upwards and consists of bracken and rough grass.

The main problem is the lack of space to run around despite the beach itself being quite wide and open. The lack of space does mean this is not a great site for spending any length of time with older children, but a pleasant time can be had relaxing by the lake and although the area can be quite busy, at least the site is well away from traffic noise and hazards.

For those feeling a little more energetic there is some good walking in this area including walks around Grasmere and Rydal Water and also on Loughrigg Fell which rises up behind the shore here.

Despite a bit of a walk from the car, this site does provide an attractive beach and fantastic Lake District scenery.

Sunshine & shelter

The shore faces north and west across the lake and is quite open so sunshine can be expected throughout the day. High ground to the west is far enough away to mean that the sun should last well into the evening.

There is no shade or shelter at the site although the trees at the western end of the beach will provide some protection in that vicinity.

Beware

- Water quality can be poor as stated on signs.

Summary

A very picturesque setting in the heart of the Lakes with a lovely beach but lack of good space and a bit of a walk.

Rydal Water

Closely related to Grasmere, Rydal Water is only about 1km downstream and again has a wonderful setting in the heart of the Lakes surrounded by great scenery.

The busy A591 somewhat spoils the northern shore but there is a popular footpath along the southern shore giving some lovely lakeshore access where the lake can be better enjoyed. Being so central the lake area can be busy and is often more pleasant away from peak times.

The nearby hamlet of Rydal has little apart from a pub and the nearest centres are either Grasmere or Ambleside.

20.   Rydal Water.

Around Grid Reference NY357060. On the southern shore of the lake.

Parking & facilities
There are no parking areas close to the site but it is possible to park at either end of the lake from where you must walk.

At the eastern end of the lake, there is a small but free car park at Pelter Bridge (NY364060), which is reached by crossing the bridge from the main A591 and taking an immediate right.

Alternatively, at the western end of the lake, there are a couple of large National Trust Pay & Display car parks either side of the main road at White Moss Common between Grasmere and Rydal, around NY350065 (free for National Trust members).

Toilets are provided by the National Trust car parks but there are no facilities on site, the nearest being in Ambleside or Grasmere village.

Access
The easiest access is from the Pelter Bridge car park from where a good track continues on for about 500m before dropping down to the lakeshore.

From the National Trust car parks take the main path across the river which then rises quite steeply and is a bit rough before dropping down to the shore of Rydal Water. This involves a walk of about 1.2km.

Description

This is a delightful shoreline access area on the picturesque Rydal Water. The site can only be accessed by walking some distance from the car but that does at least allow for some peace and tranquillity away from the busy road on the other side of the lake.

The footpath runs along the lakeshore and is normally quite busy with people doing the popular walk around Rydal Water. That walk is highly recommended and can easily be combined with a stop here for a picnic and a dip in the lake.

There is about 500m of accessible shoreline which mostly consists of a strip of flat grass between the path and the lakeshore, with a narrow shingle beach allowing easy access to the lake for paddling and bathing. There is plenty of room to spread out and some of the wider grassy areas do provide limited space to run around.

Halfway along this shore is a rocky outcrop which blocks the path and provides a bit of a challenge to clamber over and regain the path on the other side. The mountain bikes that use the route are forced around the rocks through the water which can be quite a wet experience for them!

There are also a couple of small becks that enter the lake along this shore which have good playing potential.

The shore area is very open with excellent views across the lake towards the surrounding fells making it an ideal place to spread out and relax right in the heart of the Lake District.

Sunshine & shelter

The site faces northwards across the lake but is all open so sunshine can be expected throughout the day. The sun should last well into the evening before it disappears behind the fells away to the west.

There are one or two trees but little in the way of shade or shelter.

Summary

A pleasant lakeside site with a lovely open shore and excellent views but a bit of a walk from the car.

Ullswater

A lake of many contrasts. The northern end is relatively flat and featureless, the southern end is very mountainous and spectacular, the western shore has a busy road running along it, the eastern shore is mostly roadless and quite tranquil.

There are two main centres where people tend to congregate, at Pooley Bridge and Glenridding, and these places are often best avoided on a busy summer's day.

There are no public lakeshore access points to speak of north of Howtown Bay but the rest of the lake has plenty. The main access areas are on the western shore adjacent to the road and much of this shore is accessible all the way from Gowbarrow to Glenridding providing you don't mind the crowds and the busy road. The eastern shore is much more tranquil but good access areas are limited.

21.   Ullswater at Glenridding near the steamer pier.

Grid Reference NY388167 to NY391171. In the village of Glenridding, either side of the steamer terminus area.

Parking & facilities
There are a number of Pay & Display car parks in Glenridding, the closest being at the steamer terminus where toilets can also be found.
The shoreline has several benches dotted along it with some picnic tables located outside the terminus building.
There are two food kiosks in the vicinity, one in the steamer terminus building and one at the far southern end of the site where the field meets the main road.
Additional facilities can be found in Glenridding village.

Access
The car park at the steamer terminus is adjacent to the lake with good level paths leading along the shore. If coming from the village centre, the site can be accessed from the road to the steamer pier, a distance of about 400m.

Description
This is an excellent lakeshore access area having plenty of good beaches with

acres of flat grass and easy access from the village of Glenridding.

Altogether there is about 500m of accessible shoreline stretching from the main road at the southern end of the village, NY388167, to the point where Glenridding Beck flows into the lake, NY391171.

Jenkin's Field is the land between the pier and the main road consisting of some excellent shingle beaches with a large area of flat grass behind. There is certainly plenty of space to spread out and run around with good paddling and bathing in the lake. The whole field is very open and is fenced from the road making it quite safe.

The land between the slipway at the steamer terminus and the beck is owned by the National Trust and again has some great shingle beaches with plenty of open flat grass behind. There is plenty of room to spread out and run around but this area is not fenced from the car park or access road.

This whole shore juts out into the lake on the delta feature formed by the beck and this provides some superb views in all directions, especially of the surrounding high mountains.

The new steamer terminus building has plenty of good facilities including the picnic tables on the adjacent shore and the idea of a trip down the lake on a steamer to complete your day is certainly well worth considering. It is worth mentioning that although the boats were originally built to run on steam, they are actually now diesel powered, although they are still affectionately known as 'steamers' and many of the old features are still there to be enjoyed.

There is usually plenty of boating action at this end of the lake with the steamers and the numerous sailing boats. If you fancy taking to the water yourself, there is rowing boat hire at the southern end of the site or sailing boat hire across Glenridding Beck from the site.

This area can get quite busy but with such a large access area there is plenty of room for all and the site makes an ideal location for spending a day by the lake or even just to go and relax for a while and take in the impressive surroundings whilst visiting the village.

Sunshine & shelter

The shore faces south and east here and is very open so sunshine can be enjoyed throughout the day although the nearby foothills of Helvellyn to the west will mean that the sun does not last all evening.

There are a few trees dotted along the shore to provide some shade and shelter.

Beware

- This part of the lake is normally quite busy with steamers and sailing boats and care must be taken in the water to avoid any boats which pass close to

the shore. Do not venture too far out from the shore.
- The land between the steamer pier and the beck is unfenced from the car park so care is needed with children.

Summary

An ideal site to spend a good day by the lake with plenty of opportunity for activities or relaxing in a fantastic setting.

22.   Ullswater around Mossdale Bay.

Grid Reference NY387179 to NY387181. On the western shore of the lake, off the main A592, about 1km north of Glenridding village.

Parking & facilities
There is a fairly large free car park at NY387179, situated on the opposite side of the road from the lake. Immediately to the north of this there is also limited parking along the roadside.
There are no facilities on site, the nearest being in Glenridding village.

Access
There are two good beaches here, one immediately across the road from the main car park and the other, at Mossdale Bay itself, involves walking about 100m up the road and then 30m down a rough path to the shore.
Mossdale Bay is only about 1km from Glenridding and is easily accessible on foot from the village.

Description
This site has two wonderful shore access points which are quite different but separated only by about 100m and a wooded rocky knoll.

The site immediately adjacent to the main car park is quite open with a lovely wide shingle beach and an area of flat grass where it is possible to spread out though running around can be difficult as space is limited and the site does get quite busy. There is a small beck running into the lake through the site which provides some paddling and playing potential. The beach faces southwards towards the head of the lake and there are excellent views in this direction including the high mountains beyond. Although there is some good open space, the unfenced main road runs alongside the site and is an obvious hazard.

The shore at Mossdale Bay is about 100m north of the car park and has a lovely curved shingle beach with some sloping rough grass behind and there are plenty of overhanging trees which do tend to obstruct the sun somewhat. There is plenty of room on the beach itself to spread out with limited playing area and good access to the water. This beach is set about 30m away from the road, so the road is not as obtrusive and the tranquillity of the lake along with the great views down the lake can be very much enjoyed.

Sunshine & shelter
Because of the differences in aspect and openness of the two sites there are significant differences in the sun and shade expectations.

The more southerly site by the car park faces south and east and is open so sun can be enjoyed throughout the day although the steep slopes immediately to the west will mean the sun does not last much into the evening. There are nearby trees providing some shade and shelter.

The Mossdale Bay site faces north and east and is overhung by large trees so although sunshine can be found in the afternoon it will be hard to come by. The trees will mean that the sun does not last into the evening and the site is more appealing to shade worshippers.

Beware
● The busy A592 runs close to the shore here with no barriers between the two.

Summary
Two different and picturesque sites which have limited space but excellent shorelines and views, yet still handy to Glenridding.

23.   Ullswater at Glencoyne shore access area.

Grid Reference NY387189. On the north-west shore of the lake, off the main A592, about 2km north of Glenridding village.

Parking & facilities
There is a large Pay & Display car park at the site (free for National Trust members).
There are no facilities on site, the nearest being in Glenridding.

Access
The shore is directly across the road from the car park, with the road running alongside the shore here.

Description
The beach at Glencoyne is certainly one of the best on Ullswater, with some lovely fine gravel/shingle which is as close to a sandy beach as you are likely to find in the central Lakes.
There is about 200m of directly accessible shoreline which curves right around the bay and consists of quite a wide shingle shore backed by a number of trees.
The shore opposite the car park faces north-eastwards and has a superb view

right down the lake. There are quite a number of big overhanging trees which tend to block the sun somewhat, though there are sunny gaps in-between them. Further round the bay, the shore faces south-east with excellent views across and up the lake. This beach is a bit more open with fewer trees and there is more sun to be had here.

The large expanse of open beach provides a fair amount of room to spread out and access to the water is good for paddling and bathing. Unfortunately there is little grass to speak of and the adjacent main road does slightly spoil the site with the noise and the fact that running around can be dangerous.

Access to the site certainly couldn't be easier and the great beach and setting do make a very appealing shoreline.

Sunshine & shelter
The shore generally faces in an easterly direction across the lake and there are plenty of open areas where sunshine can be enjoyed throughout the morning and afternoon. Later in the afternoon the sun will tend to be shielded more and more by the trees backing much of the site and these trees, along with the high mountains to the west, will hide the sun completely by the early evening.

There is certainly plenty of shade and shelter provided by the trees.

Beware
● The busy A592 runs alongside the shore here with no barriers between the two.

Summary
A lovely shoreline with a superb beach and views, slightly spoiled by the lack of good open space and the close proximity of the busy main road.

24.   Ullswater north of Glencoyne.

Grid Reference NY389191. On the north-west shore of the lake, off the main A592, about 200m north-east of Glencoyne car park.

Parking & facilities
There is quite a large free lay-by parking area adjacent to the road at the above grid reference.
There are no facilities on site, the nearest being in Glenridding.

Access
From the parking area there is quite a good but slightly rough and sloping path which leads about 30m down to the lakeshore.

Description
This lakeshore access area is one of several along the north-west shore of Ullswater and as with all the others there is relatively easy access to the shore from the road, but with this being a little further away from the road, the shore is a bit more peaceful.
There is about 150m of accessible shore which is fairly narrow with shingle, stone and plenty of trees behind. The shingle area is quite open and provides

room to sit with good access to the water. The area between the shore and the road is quite overgrown so there is nowhere to spread out or run around and the road is unfenced so could present a hazard to children.

The main feature of the site is the excellent view straight up the lake towards Glenridding and the high mountains beyond and despite the lack of space, it is a great place to spend some time relaxing by the lake taking in the impressive scenery.

Sunshine & shelter

The shore faces south and east up the lake and sunshine can be expected until late afternoon when the dense trees along the back of the shore will tend to hide the sun completely.

The trees will certainly provide plenty of shade and shelter at the site.

Beware

- Despite the road being set back from the shore it is unfenced and children do need to be supervised.

Summary

A very pleasant but small shoreline access area with fantastic lake and mountain views.

25. Ullswater at Aira Point access area.

Grid Reference NY399198. On the north-west shore of the lake, off the main
A592, about 200m south-west of Aira Force car park.

Parking & facilities
There is a large Pay & Display car park at Aira Force (free for National Trust
members).
There are no facilities at the lakeshore but there are toilets and a cafe at the car
park.

Access
From the car park, walk about 100m alongside the main road towards
Glenridding. On the left is a small gate and a path leads about 100m across the
field to the lakeshore. Despite the short walk the access route is good and fairly
level so should not present any difficulties.

Description
This triangular field, which is all National Trust access land, has about 150m of
excellent lakeshore access with plenty of wide open space and some superb
views.

There is a wide shingly beach area which is a little rough and overgrown in places but does provide great access to the water for paddling and bathing. Behind the shoreline is a substantial area of fairly flat grass which is also a little rough in places but provides plenty of good open space. The whole site is very open with only a few trees and there are fabulous views across the lake towards Place Fell and also up towards the head of the lake and the high mountains beyond.

The site is one of the few on this side of Ullswater which is set away from the road, so some peace and tranquillity can be enjoyed and there is also a wall between the field and the road making it quite safe for children.

If parking in the Aira Force car park it is also worthwhile to make the short walk up to the spectacular Aira Force waterfall and even on to Gowbarrow Fell where views of the area can be fully appreciated.

Sunshine & shelter

The shore faces southwards towards the head of the lake and is very open so sun can be expected throughout the day. There are high fells away to the west but the sun should still last well into the evening.

There are a number of trees scattered around the site providing plenty of shade and shelter.

Beware

- Take care when walking alongside and crossing the main road which can be busy and fast.

Summary

An idyllic site with plenty of good open space and great scenery making the short walk well worthwhile.

26.   Ullswater beneath Gowbarrow Fell.

Grid Reference NY407202 to NY415204. On the north-west shore of the lake, off the main A592, about 5km north-east of Glenridding.

Parking & facilities
There are four separate fairly small but free lay-by car parks, each about 200-300m apart, adjacent to the road.
There are no facilities on site, the nearest being in Glenridding, although there are toilets and a cafe at the nearby Aira Force car park.

Access
Each of the lay-bys has a path, up to about 50m in length, leading directly to the lakeshore. The paths are quite rough with steps and some people may find access a little difficult.

Description
This section of lakeshore is owned by the National Trust and is part of the Gowbarrow and Aira Force access areas. The National Trust shore is about 1.5km in length but the steep banks and woods make it difficult to access much of the shore except at the four recognised lay-bys where paths and steps have been made.

The area between the lay-bys and the shore tends to be mostly overgrown right down to the water's edge, but there are several small areas of open shingle in-between trees. There is little space to spread out or run around but there is good access to the water and the site is ideal if all you want to do is sit or paddle.

Despite the nearby road the shore is quite peaceful with pleasant views across the lake towards Place Fell and a nice relaxing time can be had here.

At the far south-west of the site, about 70m beyond the end lay-by at NY407202, there is a lovely shingle beach which is quite small but more open than the other access points with some excellent views looking straight up the lake towards the high mountains beyond.

Sunshine & shelter

The shore faces south and east across the lake and the more open areas can keep the sun throughout the afternoon. The many large trees overhanging and behind the site will tend to hide the sun from time to time during the day and then completely in the late afternoon.

The many trees do mean that shade and shelter can always be found.

Beware

- Although the shore is a little distance from the road, there are no barriers between the two so children need to be watched.

Summary

A picturesque and peaceful lakeshore with good views across the lake but a distinct lack of space.

27.   Ullswater at Gowbarrow Access Area.

Grid Reference NY423206 to NY425207. On the north-west shore of the lake, off the main A592, about 7km south-west of Pooley Bridge.

Parking & facilities
Parking is all free and consists of four quite large lay-by parking areas, each about 50m apart, located between the road and the shore.
There are no facilities on site, the nearest being in Pooley Bridge, although there are toilets and a cafe at the nearby Aira Force car park.

Access
Each of the lay-bys has a very short path or steps leading directly to the lakeshore. Some of the paths are a bit rough and the steps are quite steep but from the lay-by at the western end of the site, there is a good path to the shore with an easy gradient.

Description
This part of the Ullswater lakeshore is known as Gowbarrow Access Area and is about 300m in length. There is a fair amount of parking on the main road adjacent to the lakeshore making it a good place to gain easy access to the shore

although this does mean the site can be quite crowded and the main road is only a few metres away.

The shore along this stretch tends to consist of shingle beaches broken up by numerous trees, many of which have grown in seemingly impossible locations on shingle that is often under water. Much of the shingle is quite narrow between the road and the water but there are some larger shingle areas giving more room to spread out and the whole shore gives good access to the water.

There is very little grass with shingle and trees occupying any potential spaces but there is a long narrow strip of grass near to the western end of the site, squeezed between the road and the shingle.

If you can position yourself in-between the trees, the site has some pleasant views across the lake towards Hallin Fell and Martindale.

Sunshine & shelter

The shore faces south and east across the lake and despite the numerous trees, there are still plenty of more open areas where the sun can be enjoyed throughout the day.

The trees certainly provide plenty of shade and shelter, but those between the shingle and the road will make the sun increasingly scarce as the day progresses and will tend to hide it altogether come early evening.

Beware

● There is no barrier for children between the shore and the busy main road.

Summary

A pleasant lakeside area with good access where an enjoyable time can be had, but the lack of space and the proximity of the main road do detract from the appeal.

28.   Ullswater at Sandwick Bay.

Grid Reference NY426200. On the south-east shore of Ullswater, near to the hamlet of Sandwick, at the end of the minor lakeshore road from Pooley Bridge.

Parking & facilities
There is a small amount of free parking on the roadside opposite the houses at Sandwick.
There are no facilities on site, the nearest being in Pooley Bridge.

Access
From the houses at Sandwick, a footpath leads through a gate and across Sandwick Beck running north-eastwards. The path is well made but slightly rough and undulating giving a walk of about 500m down to the shore at Sandwick Bay.
Alternatively, this site can be visited if walking the popular lakeshore path between Howtown and Glenridding.

Description
This is a wonderful little bay in a great location, well away from any traffic or noise, where a good few hours can be spent by the water.
Unfortunately, parking is very limited by the houses at Sandwick but if you enjoy walking the alternative access makes a superb day out. This involves parking at Glenridding and catching the steamer to Howtown whereby a picnic

stop can be made at the bay on the walk back. This walk is in fact very popular and although road traffic isn't a problem here, there will normally be no shortage of walkers passing through along the lakeshore footpath.

The bay itself has a lovely curved shoreline with about 150m of wide shingle/gravel beach and some flat grass behind, all of which are quite open with a few trees dotted around. There is plenty of room to spread out with good paddling and bathing in the water. The views are not quite up to the standard of many other sites around the lake but are nevertheless quite pleasant looking northwards across the lake.

If you want a peaceful site away from hustle and bustle and with a nice safe environment then this site is ideal.

Sunshine & shelter
The shoreline here generally faces northwards across the lake and is open so sunshine can be expected throughout the day. There are high peaks well to the west of the site which will only hide the sun towards the end of the evening. There are a number of trees dotted along the shoreline for shade and shelter.

Summary
A very pleasant shoreline with a great beach and some grass in a lovely tranquil setting but access can be awkward.

Wast Water

This is the deepest and one of the most remote and dramatic of all the lakes. The only way of driving into the valley is from the far western side of the Lake District and despite being relatively flat and featureless at its western end, the scenery gets more and more spectacular towards the head of the lake. The famous high screes along the southern shore are particularly impressive as they tumble down over 500m from the mountain tops to the water and continue down below water level to a depth of around 80m. Further along the lake you are surrounded by several majestic tops including Sca Fell, Great Gable and Yewbarrow which all help to make the lake such an awe-inspiring place.

There is a narrow road all the way along the north-west shore which provides easy access to several excellent shoreline areas. There is a footpath along the south-east shore but the going is very rough along the screes and there are no suitable shoreline access locations.

The main centre in the valley is the village of Wasdale Head, which has limited facilities and can get quite busy during popular periods.

29. Wast Water and Over Beck at Overbeck Bridge.

Grid Reference NY168068. On the north-west shore of the lake, adjacent to the Wasdale Head road and Overbeck Bridge.

Parking & facilities
There is a sizeable public car park (donation box included) adjacent to the bridge on the opposite side of the road from the lake.
There are no facilities on site but there are limited facilities available in Wasdale Head village.

Access
The lakeshore is directly across the road from the car park with a good level route between the two.

Description
This is a wonderful lakeshore access point with some lovely open grass, shingle areas and excellent views.
Access couldn't be better with a good sized car park giving direct access to the shore. The shoreline has a fair amount of open shingle with areas of nice flat grass behind broken up by patches of bracken and gorse. There is plenty of room to spread out but running around space is a bit limited and the unfenced road is right next to the shore here.
The shore gives easy access to the water but care should be taken as the lake

does get deep quickly. Over Beck which runs into the lake here gives better paddling and playing potential and is perhaps rather safer than the lake with its shallow water gently cascading towards the lake. The beck runs for about 50m from the road bridge before entering the lake.

The whole site is open with superb views across the lake towards Sca Fell, The Screes and several other surrounding high fells.

The site provides great potential for spending a few hours by the lake in a picturesque position that is difficult to beat.

Sunshine & shelter

The lakeshore faces south-east across the lake and is very open so sunshine can be expected throughout the day. The steep slopes of Middle Fell to the west will eventually hide the sun later in the evening.

There are no trees to provide shade and shelter on the shore itself, but there are plenty of trees across the road around the car park.

Beware

- The unfenced road runs alongside the site and must be crossed to get from the car park.
- At this point it is possible to appreciate that Wast Water is England's deepest lake as the lake bed shelves quite quickly away from the shore and there is very little shallow water to paddle in. Not far from the lakeshore here the depth of water is over 60m! The beck is better for paddling being normally quite shallow with some small pools and gentle cascades.

Summary

An idyllic site adjacent to the lake and the beck with pleasant open spaces and superb views.

30. Wast Water and Nether Beck around Netherbeck Bridge.

Grid Reference NY162066 & NY163066. On the north-west shore of the lake, adjacent to the Wasdale Head road and Netherbeck Bridge.

Wast Water at Nether Beck

Parking & facilities
There is limited free roadside parking adjacent to Netherbeck Bridge but be careful not to obstruct the road.
There are no facilities on site but there are limited facilities available in Wasdale Head village.

Access
The beck can be accessed from the road on the eastern side of Netherbeck Bridge by climbing the stile over the wall. The stile is quite high and could prove difficult for some people.
The lakeshore is accessed by walking from the bridge about 150m towards Wasdale Head from where a slightly rough path runs downhill about 30m to the lakeshore.

Description

These are two very different sites which are similar in that they have been formed from the delta created by Nether Beck and are close together.

The beckside access point is small but quite secluded and pleasant being adjacent to Nether Beck between the road bridge and the lake. It is possible to park right next to the site but a wall with a high stile must be crossed to gain access. Beyond the wall is a small but nice open grassy area with patches of quite thick bracken and gorse, which is quite peaceful being hidden from the road by the wall. There is about 30m of accessible river-bank where the shallow beck flows gently past towards the lake which is about 100m downstream. There is a small shingle/stone beach area providing good paddling and playing potential and although there is very little space to run around, there is the added comfort of the wall protecting the site from the road. Despite the lack of space there is a lovely area to sit which includes a bench and there are some fine views across the lake towards the high fells and The Screes.

The lakeside site is just along the road to the east and consists of quite a large curving shingle beach backed by large trees on the shores of Wast Water. There is a fair amount of room to spread out and run around with the open shingle beach and the gently sloping grass under the trees behind. The unfenced road is only about 30m away and although it is fairly quiet it can pose a hazard to children. The beach itself provides good paddling and bathing in the lake, but the large trees behind the shingle do tend to shield the sun somewhat. The beach is quite secluded and does make a pleasant place to come and relax by the lake with some excellent views across the water towards Sca Fell and the surrounding fells.

Sunshine & shelter

The whole delta area is quite wooded although both sites do have open areas where sun can be found during the day.

The beckside area is more open to the south and west but trees to the west will tend to hide the sun in the late afternoon. The only real protection at the site is provided by the wall.

The lakeside area faces south and east across the lake but the large trees behind will tend to hide the sun completely around mid-afternoon. Shade and shelter can always be found at the lakeside.

Beware

- At the beckside site the water is normally quite shallow as it runs past in a series of small pools and gentle cascades.
- The lakeside site is open to the nearby road and care needs to be taken with children.

- At the lakeside site, some shallow water can be found near to the shore but the water soon becomes very deep and is over 70m deep not far from the shore.

Summary
A lovely little area which is quite secluded and picturesque and gives a good choice of either a beckside or lakeside recreational site.

Nether Beck

31. Wast Water along the north-west shore from Countess Beck viewpoint to Nether Beck delta.

Grid Reference NY149050 to NY160064.

Parking & facilities

There are literally dozens of small but free roadside parking areas along this stretch, but be careful not to block passing places on the single track road. The biggest parking areas are around Countess Beck Bridge at NY151053, or the big car park on the opposite side of the road to the lake at NY152055.

There are no facilities along this stretch of lakeshore and the nearest good facilities can be found at Gosforth.

Access

Many of the parking areas give almost direct access to the shore, especially those around Countess Beck. Further north the road rises slightly above and away from the lake and each parking area tends to have quite rough and fairly undefined paths leading through bracken down to the lakeshore, up to about 100m in distance.

Description

This picturesque stretch of lakeshore is almost 2km in length and there are plenty of very good open shoreline access areas which are quite peaceful with some fantastic views.

The shoreline tends to be quite rocky with small cove-like shingle beaches every so often and areas of grass and bracken behind. This pattern begins around the Countess Beck viewpoint and continues northwards to the Nether Beck delta.

It is difficult to recommend a particular point as they are all good but the shore around Countess Beck does tend to be the most popular as there is more parking and access is easier. Further north the shore access is slightly more difficult but the shore tends to more secluded and tranquil away from the road and the crowds.

Countess Beck area provides the most open space with plenty of flat grass and shingle areas on which to spread out and run around. The beck itself provides ideal paddling and playing in a slightly safer environment than the lake. At the point where the beck enters the lake there is a small 'island' which at normal lake levels is easy to get to by stepping across the conveniently placed stones. The viewpoint immediately to the south of the beck, with its prominent shelter, is easily accessed and gives exceptional views over the whole lake and right up to the head of Wasdale.

Heading northwards, as the road rises above and slightly away from the lake, there are some lovely isolated shingle beaches which can be quite easily reached though some are well hidden from the road and do require a bit of finding.

Nearing the Nether Beck delta, the road drops back down near to the lakeshore and the best beaches are left behind.

The whole shoreline is very open and there are some fabulous views both across the lake towards The Screes and up the lake towards the head of Wasdale.

Despite its beauty and great shoreline, the remoteness of this part of the Lakes does help to ensure that the area is never overcrowded and Wast Water can normally be enjoyed in relative peace and tranquillity.

Sunshine & shelter

This shoreline generally faces south and east across the lake and is very open so sunshine can be expected throughout the day. The more northern shore will begin to lose the sun in the early evening due to the steeply rising slopes of Middle Fell to the west, but much of the shore should keep the sun well into the evening.

There are no trees along this stretch at all, so very little in the way of shade or shelter.

Beware

- The unfenced road runs right along and quite close to this shoreline so children need to take care.

Summary

A superb stretch of shoreline with a series of picturesque small beaches and fabulous views allowing a good few hours to be spent by the lake.

32.   Wast Water near Wasdale Hall.

Grid Reference NY147047. On the north-west shore of the lake near to Wasdale Hall Youth Hostel.

Parking & facilities
There is room for a couple of cars by the side of the Wasdale Head road where it meets the lake at NY148048. Alternatively, there is further free parking along the road towards Countess Beck viewpoint, around NY150051.
There are no facilities on site and the nearest good facilities can be found at Gosforth.

Access
From the nearest parking area there is a fairly rough path which leads over a stile and on for about 100m through Rhododendron bushes to the lakeshore. Some people may find access a little difficult.
The alternative parking area gives an additional 400m walk along the road.

Description
This is a lovely secluded shoreline area which has some good open space and superb views.
Despite the isolation of Wast Water compared to many other parts of the Lake District, it can still be quite popular but this part of the shore is just far enough off the beaten track to retain some peace and tranquillity.

There is about 100m of pleasant shingle beach with some gently sloping but quite rough grass behind, all of which are very open. There is plenty of room to spread out with good access to the water. The views from the site are quite spectacular as it looks straight across the lake to the famous screes which can be seen in all their glory as well as some great views up towards the head of the lake. Between the site and the road is an area of Rhododendron bushes which look very attractive when flowering.

The road is about 100m away and is protected by a wall so there are no traffic hazards at the site.

The shortage of nearby parking can be a slight problem but once here a lovely time can be spent enjoying this special lake.

Sunshine & shelter
The shoreline faces south-east across the lake and is very open so sunshine can be expected throughout the day. The large trees along the top of the field will eventually hide the sun later in the evening.

There are a few bushes and small trees along the shore to provide some shade and shelter.

Beware
● If parking near to Countess Beck viewpoint, care is needed when walking along the narrow road which fortunately isn't too busy or fast.

Summary
A picturesque and tranquil site with a good open shoreline providing idyllic conditions for a few hours by the lake.

Windermere

England's largest lake at over 10 miles long and up to a mile wide. The lake is essentially an aquatic playground for all types of watersports although there are plans to impose a 10mph speed limit on the lake thus banishing speedboats and water-skiers.

The water can get very crowded and so indeed can the shore especially on the eastern side around Bowness and the northern shore at Ambleside where the majority of visitors to the area tend to congregate.

There are many good lakeshore access areas all around the lake despite the fact that much of the shore is privately owned. The more secluded shore is on the western side away from the crowds but there are some great access areas on the eastern shore where it is still possible to find some peace and tranquillity - providing you can put up with the drone of speedboats.

33.   Windermere at Borrans Park near Ambleside.

Grid Reference NY375033. At the northernmost tip of the lake between the landing jetties and the Roman Fort at Waterhead near Ambleside.

Parking & facilities
There is a large Pay & Display car park opposite the jetties at Waterhead, NY376033.
There are a number of benches and picnic tables in the park with toilet facilities and food kiosks around the car park and jetties.

Access
From the car park, Borrans Park is about 150m level walking along the lakeside road towards Ambleside.
If walking from the centre of Ambleside, there is a walk of about 1km along level roads.

Description
This is a lovely park area which has a great setting next to the lake but is still easily accessible from the Waterhead/Ambleside area.
The park has a long history dating back to Victorian times and has always been

popular with locals and tourists alike. The park looks straight down Windermere and has about 100m of attractive shoreline in the form of little cove-like shingle beaches separated by rocky outcrops. The beaches are quite short but fairly wide with some fine gravel/shingle making them very appealing with good access to the water as well.

Behind the shoreline is a thin line of trees then a large expanse of lovely open mostly flat grass with plenty of space to spread out and run around.

The park is easily accessible from the jetties if coming by boat from Bowness or Lakeside and it is also entertaining to watch the often frenzied boat activity from the park on a busy day.

This site is very handy to Ambleside and can get quite busy but it is an ideal location for spending a few hours by the lake. The nearby busy main road does not detract too much from the site and there is thankfully a big wall separating the two.

If you are feeling energetic there is also some good exploring to be done around Waterhead and Ambleside or perhaps the adjacent Roman Fort.

Sunshine & shelter

The park faces southwards down the lake and is very open so sun will last all day and well into the evening. Loughrigg Fell to the west will eventually hide the sun later in the evening.

There are quite a few trees dotted around the park providing shade and shelter.

Beware

- As the site is close to the main jetties at Waterhead, watch out for boats if bathing in the water.
- Despite the wall between the site and the road, there are a couple of open gaps where children could escape.

Summary

An excellent parkland area, very handy to Ambleside, with some lovely shingle beaches and plenty of flat open grassy areas.

34. Windermere at Jenkin Field near Ambleside.

Grid Reference NY379026. On the eastern shore of the lake adjacent to the main A591, just south of Ambleside.

Parking & facilities
Parking near to the site is almost impossible and the nearest car park is the Pay & Display opposite the ferry jetties at Waterhead, NY376033.
Toilets and food kiosks are situated around the car park but there are no facilities on site.

Access
From the car park there is a walk of about 700m to the site. Head south along the main Windermere road past the Youth Hostel and a garage which is the last building on the right. Immediately past the garage the road begins to rise up and away from the water and there is a small stile in the wall to a field by the lake. The accessible lakeshore begins here and continues on for about 300m to Holme Crag and about 150m past the crag. Once off the pavement the stile can prove a little awkward and the lakeshore path is a bit rough in places but the going is all level and should present no difficulties to able-bodied people.

Description
This triangular field jutting out into the lake is a fine and attractive site owned by the National Trust and has great views both down Windermere and across the lake to the mountains beyond.

The best beach is the one facing south which has lovely views right down the lake and about 100m of good wide open shingle with plenty of flat grass behind. The westward facing shoreline to the north of Holme Crag is also excellent, with wonderful views towards the central Lakes and plenty of shingle beaches which tend to have more trees and shelter than the south facing shore.

The whole shoreline gives easy access to the water for paddling and bathing and there is plenty of room to spread out on the shingle or on the open flat grass behind.

The main problem is the lack of close car parking meaning there is a walk involved but it is still close to Ambleside and is an ideal place to spend a few hours providing you don't mind the constant hum of traffic on the adjacent A591. Most of the shoreline is however well away from the road and is shielded by a wall so there are no safety worries.

Probably due to the access difficulty the site does tend to be ignored and is thus fairly quiet but it is certainly well worth the trip and there won't be any overcrowding.

Sunshine & shelter
The beaches face south and west across the lake and are very open so sun can be had throughout the day. The high mountains to the west are far enough away to mean the sun will last until late evening.

There are plenty of trees along the shore giving good shade and shelter which could be important with the site being quite isolated.

Beware
● If bathing be careful of the boats on the lake here, especially speed boats from the nearby Low Wood centre which seem to like this part of the lake.

Summary
A lovely uncrowded site with great open beaches and plenty of opportunity to spend a nice relaxing day but be prepared for a short walk to get there.

35.   Windermere at Brockhole Visitor Centre.

Grid Reference NY387010. On the eastern shore of the lake, off the main A591, midway between Windermere and Ambleside.

Parking & facilities
The visitor centre has a large Pay & Display car park. Toilets and picnic tables are provided near the lakeshore and additional facilities including food/drink outlets can be found around the main complex.

Access
From the car park there is a fairly level walk of about 300m along well made paths to the lakeshore. The main complex is set up above the lake and the paths to it are good but sometimes quite steep.

Description
Brockhole visitor centre is a very popular tourist attraction and has many items of interest to visitors who want to find out more about the Lake District but there is also a good lakeshore area where it is possible to spend a few relaxing hours. Brockhole has a few hundred metres of lakeshore but it is the area adjacent to the boat jetty that is most suitable for picnicking and bathing. There is about

50m of shingle and stony beach which is a little rough and overgrown but does provide good access to the lake.

Behind the beach is a line of trees and then a picnic area with several picnic tables and plenty of flat open grass on which to spread out and run around. Unfortunately, the trees hide the view of the lake from the picnic area but the views up the lake from the shoreline are superb towards the head of the lake and the mountains beyond.

Passenger boats make frequent trips to Waterhead in Ambleside from the jetty and it is perhaps worthwhile to take a boat ride and appreciate the scenery even more. The gardens at the centre also make an enjoyable potter and have many good features including an adventure playground. The centre normally closes at 5pm after which time there is no access to the grounds.

With so much to do at the centre there should be plenty of opportunity for having a pleasurable time by the lake.

Sunshine & shelter

The picnic area is surrounded by trees but is in fact quite open so sunshine can be expected throughout the day until the grounds close at 5pm. The shoreline itself is open to the west and north giving sunshine throughout the day until closing time.

There are plenty of trees around providing shade and shelter at the site.

Beware

- Watch out for boats mooring at the jetty if bathing.
- Visitor centre and grounds close at 5pm.

Summary

A great location with plenty of attractions for a family day out including a lovely picnic area close to the shore but the beach is quite small and rough.

36.   Windermere at Wray Castle.

Around Grid Reference NY376008. In the grounds of Wray Castle on the western shore of the lake, about 4km south of Ambleside.

Parking & facilities
Although the Castle is used by a private business, there is free public parking in the lower car park which is situated on the lake side of the Castle. This is signposted from the Castle gates which are on the Low Wray to High Wray road at NY371007.
There are no facilities on site, the nearest being in Ambleside.

Access
From the Castle car park there is a waymarked path which leads through a small gate to a grassy footpath which soon drops quite steeply down to the shore with a walk of about 200m.

Description
The grounds of the impressive Wray Castle form a beautiful and secluded shoreline which remains quite a secret due to its remoteness. Although it is relatively peaceful it is only a short drive from Ambleside or Hawkshead and is well worth the trip.
A fair amount of the Castle estate shoreline is wooded and makes a pleasant potter but there is about 400m of more open grassy shoreline at the southern end

of the estate which runs around to the lakeshore bridleway at High Wray Bay. This part of the shore has some fine shingle beaches with good open areas of flat grass behind though the grass does soon start to slope quite steeply further back from the shore.

The best beach is at the point closest to the Castle, around NY376009, where there is about 100m of wide and open shingle with some nice flat grass behind. The shore provides good access to the water for paddling and bathing and has attractive open views across and down the lake towards Bowness.

Moving south the shoreline has a narrow strip of shingle again with flat grass behind and some lovely views across the lake and this continues round to the picturesque High Wray Bay. The boat-house in the bay has a couple of small but appealing beaches either side with a pleasant outlook of the tiny bay.

Despite the drone of speedboats, which seem to like this part of the lake, this is a very peaceful and idyllic setting which is easily accessible and provides plenty of attractions for a few hours spent by the lake.

Sunshine & shelter
The shore here faces mostly eastwards across the lake and is quite open so sunshine can be expected throughout the day. The steep mostly wooded slopes which rise up away from the shore will tend to mean that the sun does not last much into the evening although High Wray Bay is more open to the west.

There are a number of trees dotted along the shore to provide shade and shelter.

Beware
● If bathing, watch out for the speedboats which can come close to the shore here.

Summary
A very picturesque and peaceful shoreline with plenty of good open space in a safe environment.

37.   Windermere at Red Nab.

Grid Reference SD386994. On the western shore of the lake about 1.5km south-east from the hamlet of High Wray.

Parking & facilities
There is a fairly small but free parking area adjacent to the lake at the end of the minor access road from High Wray.
There are no facilities on site and the nearest will be found in Hawkshead.

Access
The parking area is level with and immediately adjacent to the lakeshore.

Description
This is a lovely secluded but small lakeshore access area at the end of a dead end road well away from the hustle and bustle that affects much of the shore of Windermere.
This part of the lakeshore remains largely undiscovered and is a little difficult to find but providing you can reach the hamlet of High Wray, the access road is easily followed from there down to the lake.
There is very little traffic but there is a popular bridleway that leads along the

lakeshore here on its way from High Wray Bay to the ferry so there will be a number of pedestrians and cyclists passing through.

The site itself is quite small with about 50m of narrow shingle beach which does give easy access to the water for paddling and bathing. Along the back of the shingle there are a number of overhanging trees and a small stone retaining wall with the car park right behind that. There is enough open room on the shingle to spread out but very little for running around.

In-between the trees there are some pleasant open views across the lake towards Troutbeck and Windermere and despite the lack of space a good time can be had relaxing by the lake.

Sunshine & shelter

The shore faces eastwards across the lake but the line of trees along the back of the shingle will often shield the sun throughout the day although a sunny spot can always be found. The land behind the shore to the west does rise gradually and the large trees on this land will tend to hide the sun completely in the early evening.

The trees will certainly provide plenty of shade and shelter at the site.

Beware

- The shore is open to the parking area and access road but there will be very little traffic as the road is a dead end.

Summary

A secluded and picturesque site which is only small but has easy access and provides a good position to enjoy some peace and tranquillity on the shores of Windermere.

38.   Windermere at Rayrigg Meadow and Millerground.

Grid Reference SD402984 & SD402988. On the eastern shore of Windermere, about 1.5km north of Bowness, just off the main A592.

Shore at Rayrigg Meadow

Parking & facilities
There is a large Pay & Display car park at Rayrigg Meadow adjacent to the main road. Millerground is best reached from the large lay-by about 200m north of the Rayrigg Meadow car park (SD404988) where parking is free.
Rayrigg Meadow has toilet facilities, several picnic tables and a children's play area all adjacent to the car park. A barbecue area and a couple of picnic tables are provided by the lakeshore. Millerground has some benches overlooking the lake.
Further facilities are available in nearby Bowness.

Access
There is a good gently sloping path from the Rayrigg Meadow car park down to the shore which is about 150m in distance.
From the Millerground lay-by there is a rougher path leading about 200m quite steeply down to the shore.

Description

Although these two sites are separate and have different names, they are close together and being part of a continuous stretch of accessible shoreline they are considered as one site for this purpose.

Altogether there is about 700m of public access shoreline but a lot of that is quite overgrown and rocky making access difficult. There are plenty of trees all along the shoreline but there are several more open sections of beach where it is possible to sit and spread out and the best two places are the beaches adjacent to Rayrigg Meadow and at Millerground.

Rayrigg Mcadow is the more purpose built area with plenty of good facilities and a more open lakeshore which does make it quite popular. The shingle beach is about 50m long but quite wide with a couple of picnic tables and a barbecue area making an ideal place for a picnic/barbecue. There are some excellent views from the shore both across and up the lake towards the high mountains beyond. There is a general lack of open space along the shore making running around difficult but if that is a problem there is plenty of open grass and a play area up near the car park which also has several picnic tables.

Millerground, which is about 250m north from Rayrigg Meadow beach, has little open space but is quieter and has a better reputation with locals for relaxing and bathing. The shore tends to be made up of small narrow shingle beaches in-between jetties and trees and there are also some well positioned benches alongside the shoreline buildings giving superb views across the lake.

One of the main features of this shoreline is the ease of access being just off the main road near the towns of Windermere and Bowness. It is also a lovely location where the lake atmosphere can be enjoyed with great views up the lake towards the main Lake District mountains.

Sunshine & shelter

The whole shoreline faces westwards across the lake and the more open beaches at Rayrigg Meadow and Millerground can expect sunshine from late morning onwards. The remainder of the shore has quite dense overhanging trees which do tend to shield the afternoon sun somewhat. As the sun falls to the west the shore will get more and more sun until late evening when it eventually disappears behind the distant mountains to the west.

There is always plenty of shade and shelter for those who appreciate that.

Beware

- Both sites have jetties which are used by private boats so care should be taken when bathing in the water.
- The play area at Rayrigg Meadow is directly fenced from the road but is open to the car park from where the road can be reached.

Summary

A pleasant and easily accessible site with plenty of facilities and superb views making a very desirable location.

Millerground

39. Windermere at Cockshott Point, Bowness.

Grid Reference SD396964. Parkland adjacent to The Glebe in Bowness.

Parking & facilities
There is some free roadside parking on Glebe Road, which runs around The Glebe, but there is a 2hr maximum stay and available spaces are often few and far between. Alternatively, there are two Pay & Display car parks on Glebe Road or there is one on Ferry Nab Road which runs down to the car ferry.
There are some benches around the park but the nearest toilets and food/drink facilities are on Glebe Road.

Access
From Glebe Road, at the point where it swings away from the lake towards the Pitch & Putt, there is a signposted level footpath leading off into the park. From this point the lakeshore is about 200m away.
A good path also leads from the Ferry Nab car park about 300m along the lakeshore.

Description
This is a delightful parkland area with plenty of good lakeshore access and still

only a short distance from the main attractions of Bowness.

Cockshott Point is on a promontory between Bowness Bay and Ferry Nab and because of this there are some lovely views both up and down the lake. The park itself is mostly flat and has plenty of open grassy areas with some trees where it is possible to spread out and run around in safety being well away from any roads. There is plenty of wide open shingle shore all around the site giving good access for paddling and bathing, although care must be taken in the water with the many passing boats. The site does provide a great vantage point to watch the boats which squeeze between the Point and Belle Isle which is only about 150m offshore.

Considering how close the park is to the hustle and bustle of Bowness, it is surprisingly peaceful and a relaxing time can be enjoyed next to the lake.

Sunshine & shelter

The park aspect varies from facing north-west to south-west and the open grass and shingle will keep the sun throughout the day. The wooded slopes of Claife Heights across the lake to the west are far enough away to mean that the sun will last well into the evening.

There are plenty of trees dotted around the park giving good shade and shelter.

Beware

- Boats are continually travelling quite close to the shore here and despite the speed limit at this point, care must be taken if bathing.

Summary

A lovely parkland site, with some good open areas of grass and shingle, yet still very handy to Bowness.

40.   Windermere around Coatlap Point.

Grid Reference SD388959 to SD388970. On the western shore of the lake near the car ferry, just off the main B5285 Hawkshead road.

Parking & facilities
There is a fairly large Pay & Display car park at Harrow Slack (SD388959) (free for National Trust members), which is found by driving northwards along the lakeshore track from the ferry terminus and is located on the opposite side of the track from the lake. There are also limited roadside parking areas all the way along the track to the point where it enters the woods.

The alternative is to leave the car on the Bowness side of the lake and go on foot via the ferry, then walk the 700m or so along good level surfaces from the western ferry terminus.

There are no facilities on site although toilets can be found at the ferry terminus on the western shore. Bowness or Hawkshead have the nearest main facilities.

Access
All parking areas are adjacent to the track from where there is generally only a few metres fairly level walk across the grass to the lakeshore.

Description

This is a very quiet and pleasant site with plenty of good open spaces and excellent views, well away from the crowds around the lake.

Lakeshore access runs for about 1km northwards from Coatlap Point, but the Point has the easiest access being close to the car park and also has the best area of grass.

Around the Point there is a good area of open and gently sloping grass between the track and the lake where there is plenty of room to spread out and run around and also enjoy the superb open views up the lake towards the mountains beyond. There is an open shingly shore which allows easy access to the lake for paddling or bathing.

North of Coatlap Point there are some sections of shoreline which are quite narrow and overhung by trees but there are also some further open grassy areas which again provide plenty of space, great views and good access to the lake.

Towards the northern end of the site, before the track disappears into the wood, the shore is more rough and overgrown and is mostly used for boat launching and storage.

Sunshine & shelter

The site faces eastwards across Windermere towards Belle Isle and is quite open so sunshine can be expected throughout the day. The steep wooded slopes of Claife Heights immediately to the west will mean the sun does not last much into the evening.

There are always handy trees to be found for shade and shelter.

Beware

- This part of the lake has many boats moored just offshore so beware of moored and moving boats if bathing.
- If you do use the ferry to get here, make sure you don't miss the last one back, especially if on foot!
- The unfenced track runs close to the shore and is potentially a hazard but there are very few vehicles.

Summary

A peaceful site with some excellent views and good open grassy areas which provides an ideal place to come and avoid the crowds.

41.   Windermere at Beech Hill picnic site.

Grid Reference SD389921. On the eastern shore of the lake, off the main A592, midway between Bowness and Newby Bridge.

Parking & facilities
There is a large Pay & Display car park adjacent to the main road, just south of Beech Hill Hotel.
Toilets and picnic tables are provided although the nearest main facilities will be found in Bowness.

Access
The car park is immediately adjacent to the grassy mound which is the picnic site and there are good paths between the two.
The lakeshore is not far beyond but is rather more difficult to reach being about 100m down plenty of steps. Some people may find access a little difficult.

Description
This is a site of two halves with the picnic area being set a short distance away from the lakeshore and also some way above it.
The first and most obvious attraction of this site is the picnic area which is

positioned on a grassy mound and has a lovely setting overlooking the lake with extensive views towards the Lake District mountains. The mound has some quite good open grass with picnic tables dotted around the top level area and this provides an excellent position to picnic, relax and soak up the views. The grassy area is quite large so playing is possible but the steep side slopes of the mound may hinder any 'big' games.

The lakeshore is well hidden from the picnic area and is very pleasant with attractive views both up and across the lake in a peaceful setting. There is about 150m of good but quite narrow shingle beach providing easy access to the water for paddling and bathing. The beach is backed by quite dense overhanging trees and a steep slope, meaning that although there is some room to spread out on the shingle, there is a distinct lack of space to run around and there is also a shortage of sunshine.

There is no real problem with walking down to the lake and having a paddle or bathe but it is probably best to base yourself up at the picnic site because of the limited space on the shore itself.

Sunshine & shelter

The main picnic site is very open and set above the lake so sunshine can be expected all day and well into the evening. The lakeshore is lower down and well shielded by overhanging trees which will hide the midday sun and the best time to catch sun is probably later in the afternoon and evening as it falls to the west.

There are plenty of trees at both locations to provide shade and shelter.

Beware

- Signs at the picnic site state that the lake bed shelves steeply and although it does tend to shelve more steeply than at other sites around the lake, there is still a fair amount of shallow water for paddling.
- There is a fence between the picnic site and the car park but there are open gaps where children could escape.

Summary

A great place to come for a picnic with magnificent views and some fairly limited but very pleasant lakeshore access.

42.   Windermere at Fell Foot Park.

Grid Reference SD380870. At the southern end of the lake, off the main A592, about 1km north-east of Newby Bridge or 10km south of Bowness.

Parking & facilities
The park is owned and run by the National Trust and there is a large Pay & Display car park provided (free for National Trust members).
There are many other facilities on site including toilets, cafe, shop and rowing boat hire.

Access
Good paths lead from the car parks to the lakeside area, a distance of about 200m with a slight slope.

Description
This is a beautiful lakeside park location where you can easily spend a day relaxing by the water. The park is situated at the southern tip of Windermere where the lake drains into the River Leven and the water here is really the transition point between the lake and the river.
The park has vast areas of well kept grassy grounds right next to the water as

well as delightful rhododendron gardens set back from the water's edge. On a good day there are always plenty of people basking on the open grass but there is also enough space for playing games and playgrounds are provided. The main park area is well away and fenced from the main road so there should be no traffic safety worries with children. There are several picnic tables located around the park, some in shade and some not, but the grass is always a good place to spread out with a picnic.

Although much of the park is quite enclosed with plenty of bushes and trees, there are some lovely views near the water's edge looking straight up the lake to the mountains beyond

There is a small retaining wall running along the water's edge with steps leading down into the shallow water giving easy access for paddling. The water gets gradually deeper towards the centre giving good bathing. At this point the lake/river is only about 50m across and it is possible at lower levels for an adult to wade across. Perhaps because it is quite shallow the water here is often warmer than at many other locations described in this book.

With such a superb setting and so many attractions this site provides ideal conditions for enjoying a full day by the lake.

Sunshine & shelter

The site faces westwards across the lake and is mostly very open so sunshine can be expected throughout the day until the park closes at 7pm.

There are plenty of trees and bushes around providing good shade and shelter.

Beware

- The lake/river is navigable at this point and smaller boats, including powered craft, do pass quite regularly.
- The water is fairly shallow immediately offshore of the park itself but soon becomes very deep upstream and downstream of that area.
- The park closes at 7pm or dusk if earlier.

Summary

Just about perfect for a full day of enjoyment by the lake.

The Rivers

Public riverside access areas are not as common as those on the lakes and for this reason there are very few riverside locations described in the book.

A big attraction of the rivers and becks is the soothing sound and sight of the water gently cascading past which certainly enhances the appeal and helps to make the sites ideal for sitting and relaxing.

The riverside locations tend to be more suitable for paddling in a safer environment than the lakes as the depth is usually quite shallow and any deeper water is normally more obvious from the water's edge.

Some of the rivers do have deeper pools where bathing is possible and some of these are described in the book, but for the most part the rivers are normally shallow and gently flowing with perhaps small cascades which are ideal for paddling and playing.

The other main difference between the rivers and the lakes is that the character of rivers can change completely in a short space of time. The Lake District rivers are notoriously responsive to any rain and can turn from babbling becks to raging torrents sometimes in a matter of minutes. It is unlikely that people will be in the river if there is heavy rain but care should be taken if rivers do start to rise with the associated increase in depth and speed.

The book describes the rivers in normal summer conditions but if there has been any significant rain the rivers soon rise and access to them is not recommended.

43.   Barrow Beck at Ashness Bridge.

Grid Reference NY270197. About 4km south of Keswick, 700m or so up the Watendlath road from the B5289 Borrowdale road.

Parking & facilities
There is a large free car park about 50m up the road from the bridge.
There are no facilities on site, the nearest being in Keswick.

Access
From the car park, the river-bank is adjacent on the opposite side of the road although the ground is quite rough.

Description
Because of its beauty, Ashness Bridge has become very famous over the years and is the subject of many a picture postcard of the Lake District. Justifiably so with its gently cascading beck, lovely old packhorse bridge and fantastic views down the valley towards Derwent Water, Keswick, Bassenthwaite Lake and Skiddaw beyond.
Upstream of the bridge, overlooking this magnificent scene, there is a fair amount of open space on either side of the beck where it is possible to sit and

enjoy the place. The beck provides good paddling and playing with its little pools and small cascades but there is not much room to run around and the unfenced road can also be a hazard. The ground does mostly slope and is quite hard with some grass between rocks and cobbles.

The trouble with such a lovely and well known position is that it does get very busy with people stopping to admire the scene so a peaceful picnic might not be possible. However, there is room to sit back from the main crowds and although it may not be an ideal place to spend any length of time, there is still plenty of enjoyment to be had.

If you want to see an even more magnificent scene then about 800m up the road (free car park adjacent) is the fabulous Surprise View. This spectacular view over the Derwent valley is undoubtedly one of the best in the Lakes and should not be missed.

Sunshine & shelter
The beck runs in a northerly direction under the bridge and the site is quite open so sunshine can be expected throughout the day. The large trees across the road to the west do mean that the sun will tend to disappear in the late afternoon. There are some trees by the beck where shade and shelter can be found.

Beware
- The unfenced road runs past the site and some caution is needed.
- The rocks in the beck can be slippery if wet and there are one or two quite small but potentially nasty drops in the channel.
- The beck is normally very shallow with small pools and gentle cascades.

Summary
Literally a picture postcard site with magnificent views and some nice areas to sit and paddle but not much space and can get overcrowded.

44.   River Derwent at Grange-in-Borrowdale.

Grid Reference NY254175. Adjacent to the B5289 Borrowdale road at the village of Grange, about 7km south of Keswick.

Parking & facilities
There is very limited free parking by the small church at the Grange end of the road bridge into the village, or there is a small but free car park on the main B5289 just towards Keswick from the Grange turn off (NY256176).
There are toilets and food facilities in the village of Grange.

Access
The car park by the bridge is adjacent to the site with a short but quite steep path down to the river.
There is quite a rough but easy access to the river through a gap in the wall on the opposite river-bank from the village.
Access to the island is via a tricky stile from the road bridge, or simply across the shingle from the village river-bank.
If parking at the public car park on the main road, there is a walk of about 300m along the roadside path to the road bridge across the River Derwent into Grange.

Description

Grange-in-Borrowdale is a small but beautiful village where the River Derwent suddenly becomes very wide with some lovely shallow crystal clear water and large areas of shingle.

The road bridge from the Borrowdale road to the village is naturally quite long to span the wide river channel and is split into two parts with an island in the middle.

At normal levels most of the flow in the river goes through the arch furthest from the village and downstream of the bridge there is some good paddling and bathing on that side where the river forms a series of fairly shallow pools and faster moving but quite safe cascades. That side also has the largest expanse of shingle which provides plenty of space to spread out although the quite coarse surface might make it a little uncomfortable.

There is normally no flow through the arch nearest the village and this side also has some great shingle areas with a number of still pools to play in which extend upstream of the bridge towards the main river channel.

Further upstream of the shingle the water does get quite deep as the river ponds up before falling through the bridge.

The shingle basically forms part of the river bed and during a flood the whole area will be under water but at normal levels the shingle makes an ideal place to relax, picnic and paddle by the river. There are some small areas of grass on the island but other than that the shingle is really the only place to go but there is certainly plenty of it to choose from.

The fact that the site is set down in the river channel and is more or less surrounded by trees does mean there are no spectacular views, but there is a pleasant outlook including the picturesque river channel and glimpses of surrounding fells.

The valley of Borrowdale and the village can get busy in the summer but the river here provides good relaxation away from the hustle and bustle and a lovely time can be had by the water.

Sunshine & shelter

The river flows northwards at this point and much of the shingle is quite open despite being surrounded by trees so sunshine can be expected throughout the day. Trees on the western river-bank along with the nearby high fells mean that the sun will not last well into the evening.

There are plenty of trees around to provide shade and shelter.

Beware

- The river varies from deeper pools where bathing is possible to much shallower pools and small cascades. At normal levels the water is never really deep or fast enough to cause any problems though it does get a lot deeper upstream of the bridge past the shingle. There are some shallow pools on the Grange side which are away from the main flow of the river and are safer.

- Despite a wall between the river and road there are open gaps through which children can escape.

Summary

A picturesque site in a great location next to the river and the village with plenty of open space but you must like shingle!

45. River Duddon at Birks Bridge picnic site.

Grid Reference SD235995. Off the Duddon Valley road, about 2.5km south of the Wrynose Bottom/Hardknott Pass junction, or 4km north from the hamlet of Seathwaite.

Parking & facilities
There is a large free car park provided with several picnic tables overlooking the river.
There are no other facilities on site, the nearest being some 15km back down the valley at Broughton-in-Furness, although Seathwaite does have a pub at least.

Access
The river-bank picnic area is level with and immediately adjacent to the car park.

Description
This is a tranquil and picturesque picnic site which has been created by the Forestry Commission right next to the lovely River Duddon.
Although the valley is quite wooded here, the site itself is very open and pleasant with some attractive views of the surrounding high fells including Harter Fell which rises steeply up from across the river.
The river normally cascades quite gently past the site and is crystal clear having just begun its trip down Dunnerdale from Wrynose Bottom. There are no pools

as such but paddling is possible with the shallow water and stony bed.

Between the car park and the water are situated several picnic tables with some rough gently sloping grass leading down to the water, but there is not much room for running around and the open car park and road could also be a hazard.

From here, it would also be worthwhile walking southwards down the road for about 200m to the point where the river runs through a very confined gorge and is traversed by the old stone bridge. The river is extremely deep through the gorge but still crystal clear and very picturesque.

This site is also a popular starting point for the ascent of Harter Fell which is a good walk for those feeling more energetic.

The site is probably more suitable for sitting and relaxing with limited playing and paddling but is nevertheless a lovely place to come and enjoy this remote and beautiful area.

Sunshine & shelter

The picnic site faces northwards across the river but is quite open to the south and west so will keep the sun throughout the day. The bulk of Harter Fell to the west means that the sun will not last all evening.

There are a few trees dotted around the site providing some shade and shelter.

Beware

- The site is unfenced from the car park and the road which are normally quiet but care is needed.
- Being so close to the headwaters, the river can rise very quickly given any rain.
- At the picnic site the river is normally quite shallow and not more than about a couple of feet deep.

Summary

A remote site which has been nicely transformed to a pleasant and tranquil picnic area, ideal for relaxing and enjoying the surroundings.

46.   River Esk at Forge Bridge.

Grid Reference SD149995. Off the Eskdale Green to Ulpha road, about 1km south-east of Eskdale Green.

Parking & facilities
There is quite a large free lay-by car park on the south side of the bridge.
There are no facilities on site, the nearest being in Eskdale Green.

Access
The river-bank is reached through a gap in the wall with a small stile, immediately adjacent to the car park.

Description
This site consists of a single large but fairly shallow pool on the River Esk, directly downstream of the road bridge.
The River Esk at this point has levelled out considerably heading away from the high Lake District mountains and is quite slow and meandering as it nears the estuary at Ravenglass which is only a few kilometres downstream.
On the opposite side of the wall from the car park there is a small but open area of good grass adjacent to the river which is ideal for sitting on but too small for running around. The views are quite pleasant looking across open fields towards the surrounding fells.
Downstream of the grassy area in the river channel, a large bank of stones has

built up which at normal river levels is exposed and this effectively holds back the river to form the pool. The bed of the pool shelves gradually making it ideal for paddling near the edge or bathing further in. The large stony area also provides some playing potential but is too rough for running around on.

Being so handy to the road this site does get quite busy but provides a pleasant place to relax and have a splash around.

Sunshine & shelter
The grassy area faces northwards across the river but is very open to the south and west so will get the sun throughout the day and almost until sunset.

There is a solitary tree on the grassy area but its high branches will provide little protection. The high wall will provide some shelter if needs be.

Beware
- The site is protected from the road by a large wall but the stile in the wall is open and children could potentially escape.
- Downstream of the pool the water is quite fast moving as it falls past the stony area and could be dangerous.
- The pool is normally not much more than about one metre deep at its deepest point.

Summary
Not an ideal site to spend any length of time being fairly small and often crowded but it is good for a short stop and bathe.

47.   River Mite at Miterdale Forestry Commission picnic site.

Grid Reference NY146012. Off the main Eskdale Green to Santon Bridge road, about 1.5km north-east of Eskdale Green.

Parking & facilities
There is a large free parking area at the site although the track from the main road is quite tortuous being about 1.5km long and very narrow with few passing places. This track leaves the main road at the school around NY136002.
There are no facilities on site, the nearest being in Eskdale Green.

Access
The parking area is adjacent to the river and the site is all level with a good surface.

Description
This is a very secluded and peaceful site in a lovely woodland setting being well off the beaten track up a narrow dead end road in the quiet valley of Miterdale. The site is not signposted at all from the main road and the access track is quite long and narrow, but this does mean that few people find the site and an enjoyable time can be had enjoying the picturesque setting away from the crowds.

The site is positioned just before the access track crosses the river and there is a large area of good open level grass where it is possible to park with plenty of room to spread out and run around.

There is about 50m of accessible river-bank with a small retaining wall where the pretty River Mite flows gently past. The shallow water and rocky bed make it ideal for paddling and playing although there is not enough depth for bathing. There is a pleasant natural outlook with woodland surrounding the majority of the site apart from the upstream direction where there are attractive open views and the bulk of Sca Fell is quite prominent in the distance.

Sunshine & shelter
The river flows in a south-westerly direction past the site and the grassy area is very open so sunshine can be expected throughout the day. The trees on the opposite river-bank will tend to hide the sun in the evening.

Despite being mostly surrounded by trees, there are no trees on the site itself to provide shade or shelter.

Beware
- The site is open to the road and the car park but there are so few cars there is no big danger.
- At normal summer levels the river is quite shallow and safe as it flows gently past the site.

Summary
A very pleasant and peaceful site in a lovely woodland setting providing a good place to relax and paddle away from the crowds.

48.   River Rothay at White Moss Common.

Grid Reference NY348064. Off the main A591 midway between Grasmere and Rydal.

Parking & facilities
There are a couple of large National Trust Pay & Display car parks either side of the main road around NY350065 (free for National Trust members).
Toilets are provided on site but there are no other facilities, the nearest being found in Grasmere village.

Access
From the car parks there are good level paths leading about 200m to the river.

Description
The River Rothay begins high up in the hills to the north of Grasmere and flows quickly down into the lake, then on to Rydal Water before continuing down into Windermere at Ambleside. Between the lakes of Grasmere and Rydal Water there is a short stretch of very picturesque river and just before it enters Rydal Water is a lovely little access area.
There is a large expanse of open flat grass with a few benches adjacent to the

river where it is possible to spread out and run around. The accessible water's edge is about 30m in length and has some boulders protecting the river-bank giving reasonable access to the water. The river is normally quite safe with some shallow pools and gentle cascades giving good paddling though there is not enough depth for bathing. The site is some distance from the road with a wall between the two so there are no traffic hazards.

Despite being an open area, it is actually surrounded by trees which do tend to obstruct any views giving the site a 'clearing in the woods' feel.

There are numerous paths running around this area and it does get quite busy with people walking and exploring. If you are feeling energetic there is certainly plenty of opportunity for a stroll perhaps around Rydal Water or Grasmere or up nearby Loughrigg Fell from where there are some excellent views.

Given the ease of access to the site and the good grassy areas on which to relax, this site provides plenty of attractions for a pleasant few hours by the water.

Sunshine & shelter
The site faces southwards across the river and is quite open so sunshine can be expected throughout the day. The large trees to the west do mean that the sun will not last much into the evening and there are certainly plenty of trees providing shade and shelter for those who need it.

Beware
- If parking on the opposite side of the road from the site, the road is busy and dangerous to cross.
- Adjacent to the site, the river is normally quite shallow and not more than about a couple of feet deep.

Summary
A pretty little site with easy access and some good open grass where a very pleasant time can be spent relaxing by the river.

49.   Watendlath Tarn and Beck at Watendlath.

Grid Reference NY275163. At the hamlet of Watendlath, about 8km south of Keswick, signposted from the B5289 Borrowdale road.

Parking & facilities
There is a large National Trust Pay & Display car park in the hamlet of Watendlath (free for National Trust members), where there are also toilet facilities and a cafe.

Access
The tarn and beck are easily reached from the car park via good level paths, less than 100m walk.

Description
The tiny ancient hamlet of Watendlath is in a fantastic setting quite high up in a small hanging valley at the point where Watendlath Beck flows out of Watendlath Tarn on its journey towards Lodore Falls and Derwent Water.
Despite being at the end of a tortuous dead end road which can be quite busy and is only single track with passing places, the trip is definitely worthwhile just to relax by the beck or tarn and soak up the surroundings.
The tarn itself is a popular fishery and bathing is not recommended but paddling is possible from the shore around the beck outlet where there is some narrow shingle with grass behind.

Downstream of the ugly nets that prevent fish escaping the tarn, the shallow beck is very attractive and provides good paddling and playing as it flows gently towards the cascades further down.

There are some great places to sit and relax including the shingle and grass shore of the tarn adjacent to the beck, or the grass on either side of the beck upstream of the pretty little footbridge, or the grass around the rocky outcrop which overlooks the hamlet on the opposite side of the beck downstream of the footbridge. All are quite open with fine views and have some good grassy areas on which to spread out but very little room for running around.

Although the beck can be accessed downstream of the footbridge, there are some quite big drops and the best place for paddling is between the footbridge and the fish nets.

Despite its popularity the area retains its charm and a lovely time can be had relaxing by the water enjoying the ambience of this ancient place.

Sunshine & shelter
The whole area is very open and sunshine can be expected throughout the day although the higher fells to the west do mean the sun will not last all evening. There are a few small trees dotted around to provide shade and shelter.

Beware
- Between the fish nets and the footbridge the beck is very shallow and slow but there are some big falls in the beck downstream of the footbridge.

Summary
An idyllic little hamlet with a picturesque tarn and beck providing excellent relaxation and good paddling.

50.   Yewdale Beck at Low Tilberthwaite.

Grid Reference NY307010. Adjacent to the minor Tilberthwaite road, about 4km north from Coniston village.

Parking & facilities
There are a couple of large free car parking areas at the site, either side of the bridge over the river.
There are no facilities on site, the nearest being in Coniston village.

Access
The car parks are adjacent to the river giving direct level access to the river-bank although a small stile must be crossed to reach the main part of the site.

Description
This is a great little access area with some good open flat grass and plenty of wide and shallow water to play in.
From the main car park before the bridge, the best section of river-bank is directly across the road through the gap in the wall where there is an area of flat grass on which to spread out but not much room to run around. The grass is surrounded by bracken and leads down onto the stony river bed area which is quite large and abounds in bits of slate washed down from the old quarries upstream of the bridge.
The history of this area is all too evident with dozens of old slate piles scattered

around the landscape, the one next to the main car park being the most obvious. The river channel is actually a bit of a scar on the landscape with the stone and slate from the old quarries being strewn across the whole channel but nevertheless it does provide good paddling and playing. The slate is quite raw and has been smoothed over the years so is not as sharp as some cut pieces are. The steep slopes of the mighty Wetherlam rise up directly to the west of the site, but the area is quite open in the other directions and there is an attractive outlook of the surrounding hills.

Mainly due to its beauty and ease of access from the central Lakes, Tilberthwaite can be quite busy with walkers and sightseers alike, but this site does provide scope for a few hours spent relaxing and paddling in a very pleasant setting.

Sunshine & shelter
The site is very open and sunshine can be expected throughout the day. The high steep slopes immediately to the west will tend to hide the sun in the early evening.

There are no trees around the site although there are some around the car park on the opposite side of the river.

Beware
- The open gap in the wall does mean that children can get to the road but there is very little traffic along the minor dead end road.
- The nearby slate piles might look fun playing but they are very steep, loose and dangerous.
- At normal summer levels the river is quite shallow and not too fast as it flows gently past the site.

Summary
A lovely little site in a pleasant setting with easy access, a nice area of grass and good playing in the beck.